Gregory Maertz

Children of Prometheus:
Romanticism and Its Legacy

Essays in Literature, Philosophy, and Cultural Politics

/

Gregory Maertz

CHILDREN OF PROMETHEUS: ROMANTICISM AND ITS LEGACY

Essays in Literature, Philosophy, and Cultural Politics

Bibliographic information published by the Deutsche Nationalbibliothek
Die Deutsche Nationalbibliothek lists this publication in the Deutsche
Nationalbibliografie; detailed bibliographic data are available in the Internet at
http://dnb.d-nb.de.

Bibliografische Information der Deutschen Nationalbibliothek
Die Deutsche Nationalbibliothek verzeichnet diese Publikation in der Deutschen Nationalbibliografie;
detaillierte bibliografische Daten sind im Internet über http://dnb.d-nb.de abrufbar.

Cover image: *Prometheus bringt den Menschen das Feuer* (1817) by Heinrich
Füger (1751–1818). Source: Museumslandschaft Hessen Kassel.

ISBN-13: 978-3-8382-1591-4
© *ibidem*-Verlag, Stuttgart 2021

Printed in the United States of America

For

Natasha Eve Coats

&

Wanda Irene Lani Len Parker

Contents

Contents

Preface and Acknowledgements

Over the years, colleagues, students, and friends have urged me to collect and publish in one place essays that were scattered in various journals and anthologies, and thus, with this volume, I have done so. From early attempts at emulating the belletristic verve of my first teachers—Erich Heller, Harry Levin, and W.J. Bate—to more rigorously scholarly work, which incorporates the example of my Ph.D. mentors, James Engell and Jerome H. Buckley, these essays map the intellectual journey taken from my undergraduate days through graduate school and into the early years of my academic career. Besides reflecting the personal evolution of one who owed his rescue from a chaotic childhood to courses on literature and art into a politically engaged scholar on the faculty of a minority-majority urban university, these essays represent a sustained effort to understand the revolutionary cultural dynamism unleased by Romanticism which continued to be felt for more than a century.

Beginning with an assessment of Arthur Symonds's critique of Sir Thomas Browne, "The Paradox of Faith in Sir Thomas Browne and Kierkegaard," which resonates with the values of the Aesthetic Movement (inspired by Victorian admiration of the sonically lush poetry of John Keats), and then culminating in "From Translation to Authorship: Anglophone Women Writers and Goethe," a survey of the formative impact of Goethe's works in Britain and America, the essays in between mark some of the forms in which the legacy of Romanticism was expressed in English, German, and Russian. The first five essays are categorized as "comparative" because in each of them one or more works are compared with others. In all of them, acknowledged or unconscious affinity—between Browne and Kierkegaard, William Godwin and his daughter Mary Shelley, Tolstoy and Schopenhauer, the poet Rainer Maria Rilke and the sculptor Auguste Rodin, and the poets Osip Mandelstam, Rilke, and David Jones—forms the basis for ideological and formal comparison. The last four essays are organized under the heading of "cultural politics." Each of them seeks to illuminate and better understand the fusion of literature, philosophy, and politics associated with writers in the Godwin Circle in Britain and Transcendentalism in New England with an appreciation of the central role that anglophone women writers played in the reception of Goethe.

Uniting the diversity of cultural activity discussed and analyzed in this collection of essays is the Titan god Prometheus, in whose double aspect as "fire bringer" (Pyrphoros) and "creator" (Plasticator) of humankind out of earth and water is embodied the qualities synonymous with the Romantic Movement—rebellion, defiance, suffering, endurance, and martyrdom, which are combined with creativity and altruism. Above all, Prometheus, who animated the homunculi that he molded with the fire that he had previously stolen from heaven, is a symbol of the struggle against arbitrary, abstract, oppressive authority, which includes rejection of the international Enlightenment consensus on taste, decorum, and acceptance of hereditary autocratic rule. The Promethean fire that energizes and gives rise to much of the cultural production discussed in this book was generated by German writers and thinkers—Kant, Goethe, Schopenhauer, and Nietzsche—who inspired and empowered writers in combination with the revolutionary political, social, and cultural forces of liberation unleased in the American colonies in 1776 and in Paris in 1789. The resulting literary and philosophical works are the figurative offspring of Prometheus signaled in the title of this book.

The research represented in these pages was generously funded by an I.A. Levin Fellowship at Harvard University, an Andrew W. Mellon Postdoctoral Fellowship at Washington University, and a Jackson Fellowship at the Beinecke Library. Early versions of these essays appeared previously, and the author and publisher are grateful to the editors of *The University of Mississippi Studies in English*, the *Wiener Slavistisches Jahrbuch*, the *European Romantic Review*, the *SB Academic Review*, and *1650–1850* for permission to publish revised versions here. Unless otherwise noted, all translations are my own. I wish to thank Valerie Lange and Malisa Mahler at ibidem for their editorial and design expertise. As ever, I am profoundly indebted to my colleagues and students in the English Department at St. John's University for both moral and material support.

Cider Creek House
Griggstown, New Jersey

Here I sit and form
A man like myself;
A race like me,
To suffer and to weep,
And have enjoyment,
And to despise,
As I do, thee.

—*Johann Wolfgang von Goethe, "Prometheus" (1785)*
(translated by Henry Crabb Robinson)

Part I

Essays in Comparative Literature and Ideas

1 The Paradoxes of Faith in Sir Thomas Browne and Kierkegaard

> "How shall the dead arise, is no question of my faith; to believe only possibilities, is not faith, but mere philosophy."
>
> *Religio Medici*, Section 48

In an essay on Sir Thomas Browne (1605–1682), the great Victorian critic John Addington Symonds (1840–1893) remarks on a salient feature of *Religio Medici* (1642–43): "There is a sustained paradox in his thought which does not seem to belong to the man so much as to the artist."[1] Here Symonds verges on—but, as we shall see, just misses—a profound insight, characteristic of the Aesthetic Movement and the followers of Oscar Wilde (1854–1900) and Walter Pater (1839–1894). He removes the burden of analysis from psychology and biography to form and style. That he should do so reflects the aversion of Symonds's time to religious orthodoxy and its distrust of writers, such as Browne, who profess strong religious faith.

In Browne's case, one cannot immediately fault the critics for turning to his writings and giving only an impatient, sidelong glance at the author's life and beliefs. After all, Browne's uneventful career offers precious few insights into his writings. He was neither an iconoclastic pamphleteer turned epic poet nor tormented cleric who charted the dark nether regions of despair. Instead, he was a contemplative, variously learned country doctor, who devoted the leisure hours of his short-lived bachelorhood to the composition of his spiritual autobiography. Symonds's remark seems appropriate, then, and justified. Justified also then are the many studies of Browne's prose style. Inspiring many of these efforts is the formalist credo which states the impossibility of discussing the religious

---

1   Quoted by Austin Warren, "The Style of Sir Thomas Browne," *Kenyon Review* (13): 674–687 (678).

beliefs and moral values underpinning much serious literature: "something which, in its very essence, is too subtle and elusive to admit of definition."[2] This is an untenable position to defend. However difficult or offensive it might be, for some, to discuss these issues, only in so doing does one acquire the means of judging the suitability of the style adopted by the author and of unriddling what might otherwise remain a torturous labyrinth of language surrounding a mysterious web of ideas. Many forget that a supremely successful style is usually accompanied by equally compelling thoughts. Indeed, one is the "litmus test" of the other; a writer could not be said to employ a "good" or "interesting" style if his thoughts are muddled, or vice versa. Therefore, it is indefensible to justify, as many critics have, a preference for formalist criticism by appealing to the catch phrases of the "know-nothing" school of literary criticism. It is a fool's errand to assert that "the medium is the message" or that style is "the last most detailed elaboration of meaning" and expect to make oneself understood or arrive at a deep understanding of a literary work.[3] To do so is to abandon the primary responsibility and the *raison d'etre* of the literary critic: the elucidation of meaning in a work of art.

For obvious reasons, it is easier to discuss an essay or a poem of more recent vintage than an older one. The latter case requires a more strenuous exercise of the sympathetic imagination and the historical understanding than the former. Moreover, it may also involve a consideration of such "difficult" matters as belief and value, which still retain importance for writers of an age perhaps more innocent than ours. Attempts at bridging the gap between "the divided and distinguished worlds" of the past and present are often regarded by partisans of formalism as essays into the "history of ideas," as if to imply purity of motives as well as it has become an

---

2   Norton R. Tempest, "Rhythm in the Prose of Sir Thomas Browne," *Review of English Studies* (3): 308–318 (318).

3   The latter is William K. Wimsatt, the former is Marshall McLuhan.

act proscribed by rigid taboos. Making an excursion into the sensitive areas of thought and belief is to venture into forbidden territory. Of course, there is no denying that the task facing historical-humanistic scholarship becomes increasingly beyond our strength. It is not that, over time, the burden of historical facts becomes ever more cumbersome, but rather the longer ideas are allowed to lie fallow the more difficult it is to restore them imaginatively to common usage as accoutrements of the modern mind, even for as long as a brief literary exercise. But even a failed attempt to treat an idea sympathetically, infusing it with the credibility and the truth it enjoyed in the writer's mind, is preferable to a stylistic analysis which avoids the ideas expressed on the printed page, or treats them with derision or condescension.

Let us return to Symonds's remark on the probable source of paradox in *Religio Medici*: It "does not seem to belong to the man so much as to the artist." In the preface "To The Reader" in the authorized edition of 1643 Browne seems to support this conclusion by inserting the following proviso: "There are many things delivered Rhetorically, many expressions therein merely Tropicall, and as they best illustrate my intention; and therefore also there many things to be taken in a soft and flexible sense, and not to be called unto the rigid test of reason."[4] Browne wrote this, no doubt, to avert the criticism of those who might take exception to his "sundry particularities and personall expressions." (3) Just to be safe he reminds the reader that "what is delivered therein was rather a memoriall unto me than an example or rule unto any other," whose "intention was not publick." (3) Instantly, one wonders how seriously these qualifications are meant to be taken. Should the reader not beware of falling prey to Browne's ironic, conciliatory manner in the "To The Reader" (which follows the composition of *Religio Medici* by a decade), thereby suspending his judgment before examining the

---

4   Sir Thomas Browne, *Religio Medici* (New York: Collier, 1909), The Harvard Classics, Vol. 4, 3–4. Hereafter intra-textual references are to this edition.

main body of meditations? That Browne dons a shy, self-effacing mask is not owing to his embarrassment over a callow enterprise of his youth. Undoubtedly, he is aware of the difficulties involved in appreciating some of his conclusions, which are based on the immaterial foundation of religious conviction and tend to follow the suprarational dictates of faith. What are Browne's half-ironical strictures if not warnings to the reader that a supernatural logic has endued his meditations?

The reader has, it seems, two choices. Either they take Browne at his word and agree not to submit these "private conceptions" to scrutiny. This is the stance of formalism. Or, if the reader has it in mind to ignore Browne's mature proviso and sets out to identify the pattern in Browne's skein of thoughts, they risk getting caught in the snares of Browne's paradoxes. That is, unless the reader succeeds beforehand in ferreting out the source of paradox in Browne's meditations.

Perhaps, "the sustained paradox in his thought" has its origin not in Browne the artist, but rather in Browne the religious thinker? All great art (and, for that matter, every human order stabilized by tradition) rests on a fundamentally fixed correspondence between the answers that may be given on varying levels of profundity and with varying degrees of precision, but they are all recognizable by their basic color as the more or less right answers. Indeed, the imagination seeks out new waters in lands which have long remained inaccessible and unexplored, but there will be a place for them, hitherto left blank, on the maps of the familiar world. In *Religio Medici* we confront one such remote sphere where we survey the inner landscape of religious experience. To be sure, there are some important resemblances shared by aesthetic and ethical-philosophical (or religious) modes of expression and understanding. Both depend on the synthesizing power of the imagination, "the faculty . . . by which we unite the broken and dispersed images of the world into a harmonious poetic symbol . . . . The power of subjecting the less to the greater reality, of associating the outer with the inner, and thus of finding through the many that return to the one."[5]

In *Religio Medici*, the "religion of a physician," the strands of poetry and philosophy are woven together to form a double-layered fabric, which shows on one side the pattern of paradox, and, on the other, the union of contraries. W.P. Dunn ascribed this power of integration to Browne the "natural believer, who really knew that the intellect is not the only road to truth, and who by virtue of that instinct managed to unify the world."[6] The synthetic tendency of Browne's mind, which first isolates and then yokes such opposites as faith and reason, good and evil, art and philosophy, Christianity and paganism, the universal and the particular, angel and human being, is captured in a memorable passage in Section 34 of *Religio Medici*:

> We are only that amphibious piece between a corporall and spirituall essence, that middle forme that linkes those two together, and makes good the method of God and nature, that jumps not from extreames, but unites the incompatible distances by some middle and participating natures . . . (32)

Human beings occupy the middle position between heavenly benediction and earthly squalor. Equidistant from resurrection and damnation, each person is "that great and true Amphibium, whose nature is disposed to life not only like other creatures in divers elements, but in divided and distinguished worlds." (32)

It is necessary only to cite the *Dialogues* of Plato or the biblical parables of Søren Kierkegaard (1813–1855) in order to suggest the rich allusiveness, the play of irony, and the dramatic tension that belong to both strictly literary works and some philosophical tracts. Even if Samuel Taylor Coleridge's appraisal of Browne's meta-

5   Paul Elmer More's description of the "esemplastic power" of Samuel Taylor Coleridge's imagination, in *Shelburne Essays, Studies of Religious Dualism, Sixth Series* (Boston and New York: Houghton Mifflin Company/The Riverside Press Cambridge, 1909), 167.

6   W.P. Dunn, *Sir Thomas Browne: A Study in Religious Philosophy* (Minneapolis: University of Minnesota Press, 1950), 46.

physics is not the last word on the subject, his famous remark on *Religio Medici* underscores its uncertain position in the hierarchy of literary genres. Coleridge (1772–1834), the great Romantic poet and critic, argues that Browne's book should be considered "in a dramatic, and not in a metaphysical view, as the sweet exhibition of character and passion, and not as an expression or investigation of positive truth."[7] That is to say that one may still find pleasure in reading *Religio Medici* in spite of Browne's obtruding philosophical preoccupations. It is neither to deny the importance of Browne's ideas nor relegate them to a dark lumber room in the mansion of literature.

The case of Kierkegaard offers an especially illuminating parallel to Browne. Not only does he disclaim responsibility for his books far more vehemently than Browne; he goes so far as to disguise them as anonymous epistles and religious parables, and then published them under a pseudonym. Nevertheless, no one would dispute the seriousness or the enduring relevance of the disinherited offspring of his mind. In addition, Kierkegaard is recognized as one of the masters of Danish prose. And yet, at the first sign of ambivalence—just a sentence or two written in a tone of mild reproof against the enthusiasms of his youth—many English critics are prepared to ignore Browne's meditations altogether, as though unaware that the style and tone of *Religio Medici* are derived from his religious temperament and concerns. For example, Edward Dowden argues that Browne's work is "not modeled on the articles of a creed, but is far more the exposition of a religious temper; it concerns itself with the Christian graces."[8] Furthermore, Kierkegaard knew the contradictions of logic and willing lodged in faith as well as the difficulties encountered in sustaining the irrational premises of belief against the visible evidence of natural laws. For

---

7   Quoted by Robert Sencourt, *Outflying Philosophy: A Literary Study of the Religious Element* (London: Simpkin, Marshall, Hamilton, Kent & Co., 1923), 250.

8   Edward Dowden, *Puritan and Anglican: Studies in Literature* (New York: Henry Holt and Company, 1901, 2nd ed.,), 46.

Kierkegaard, "faith is not an aesthetic emotion, but something far higher . . . it is not an immediate instinct of the heart, but is the paradox of life and existence," the yoking of the particular and the universal in the relationship of worshipping believer and adoring God.[9] Kierkegaard's faith, as well as Browne's, rests upon "a paradox, inaccessible to thought." For, in Browne's phrase, "to credit ordinary and visible objects is not faith, but perswasion." (11) In his parable of Abraham and Isaac upon Mount Moriah, Kierkegaard identifies the man of faith as him "whose life is not merely the most paradoxical that can be thought but so paradoxical that it cannot be thought at all. He acts by virtue of the absurd,"[10] as Browne does when he pursues his reason "to an *O altitudo*." (11)

Kierkegaard defines the "absurd" as "not one of the factors which can be discriminated within the proper compass of the understanding." It is a mystery. And the mystery of faith is comprehended in the paradox that "with God all things are possible."[11] Browne is aware that the intoxicating anthropomorphism of Parmenides, who taught that "man is the measure of all things," blinds us to God's omnipotence. "We doe," Browne scolds the reader, "too narrowly define the power of God, restraining it to our capacities." (28) Indeed, "our understanding," in Browne's epistemology, "is dimmer than Moses's Eye." (14) Unwavering faith is impossible without first submitting reason to rigorous discipline. In Section 10 of *Religio Medici* Browne describes the reinforcement of faith as the process of taming the unruly flights of reason: "For by acquainting our reason how unable it is to display the visible and obvious effects of nature, it becomes more humble and submissive unto the subtleties of faith; and thus I teach my haggard and unreclaimed reason to stoope into the lure of faith." (12) Browne does not believe in what is believable to his senses. He believes in the apparently

---

9   Søren Kierkegaard, *Fear and Trembling and the Sickness Unto Death*. Trans. Walter Lowrie (Princeton: Princeton UP, rev. ed., 2013), 59.

10   *Ibid.*, 47.

11   *Ibid.*, 67.

preposterous. According to him, it is "no vulgar part of faith, to believe a thing not only above, but contrary to reason and against the arguments of our proper senses." (12) And it is his believing itself that becomes believable in the act of worship. In a different sense from that which is cited by his critics, like John Addington Symonds, Browne's ideas are utterly false. This sense of falsity is, however, not derogatory. There is a kind of falseness which, quite legitimately, affords the most refined aesthetic pleasure: it is enjoyed at that point where consistently sustained belief in the absurd assumes the semblance of spontaneity, and the most elaborate magical procedure, Browne's prose style, conjures the appearance of the naively miraculous.

2 Intertextual Dialogue: Father and Daughter Novelists

> "A new species would bless me as its creator and source; many happy and excellent natures would owe their being to me. No father could claim the gratitude of his child so completely as I should deserve theirs."
>
> Mary Shelley, *Frankenstein, or the Modern Prometheus*

> "The importance of struggling with another's discourse, its influence in the history of an individual's coming to ideological consciousness, is enormous. One's own discourse and one's own voice, although born of another or dynamically stimulated by another, will sooner or later begin to liberate themselves from the authority of the other's discourse."
>
> Mikhail Bakhtin, *"Discourse in the Novel"*

A brief survey of literary history in the late eighteenth and early nineteenth centuries yields several prominent examples of intertextual dialogue: James Boswell's *Life of Samuel Johnson* (1791), the collaboration of Johann Wolfgang von Goethe (1749–1832) with Friedrich Schiller (1759–1805) in the journals *Die Horen* (1795–1797) and *Musenalmanach* (1796–1800) and then again with C.M. Wieland (1733–1813) in *Taschenbuch auf das Jahr 1804,* and Samuel Taylor Coleridge's controversial appropriations of German sources in *Biographia Literaria* (1817). Dialogue in these works reflects a process fraught with more complexity than the term usually implies, since the emergence of each new text presupposes a struggle with more authoritative discourse. There are enough additional examples, such as the Schlegel-Tieck translation of Shakespeare (1797–1801, 1810), William Wordsworth and Coleridge's *Lyrical Ballads* (1798), and J.P. Eckermann's *Gespräche mit Goethe* (1836–48), to suggest that intertextual dialogue is one of the paradigmatic modes of Romanticism. These examples also illustrate Mikhail Bakhtin's characterization of literary history as "an arena of struggle constantly being waged . . . against various kinds and degrees of authority": the young Schiller and the amanuensis Johann Peter Eckermann (1792–1854) with Goethe, Boswell with Johnson, the "Great Cham," Coleridge (1772–1834) with Immanuel Kant (1724–1804) and F.W.J. Schelling (1775–1854), and the translators Friedrich Schlegel (1772–1829) and Ludwig Tieck (1773–1853) with the works of William Shakespeare.[1]

For Bakhtin the generic locus of this struggle is the novel and an intertextual dialogue that exemplifies the effort to achieve individuated discourse during the Romantic Period is exemplified by Mary Shelley's *Frankenstein, or the Modern Prometheus* (1818) and William Godwin's *St. Leon: A Tale of the Sixteenth Century* (1799). The intertextual ligatures connecting these texts have previously been acknowledged, but never fully revealed.[2] The present discussion is built on this previously unvisited site and is intended to satisfy two objectives: first, to suggest that *St. Leon* is the primary precursor text with which Shelley engaged in intertextual dialogue during the composition of *Frankenstein;* and secondly, as a re-writing of Godwin's novel, *Frankenstein* illustrates the dialogic progression from Shelley's appropriation of her father's discourse to the emergence of her own authorial originality. Seen from this perspective, the novel functions as an allegory of its author's education and literary apprenticeship. Moreover, intertextual dialogue between *Frankenstein* and *St. Leon* imposes a slight modification on Harold Bloom's paradigm of influence. Here, and in some of the examples

---

1   Mikhail Bakhtin, *The Dialogic Imagination: Four Essays*. Ed. Michael Holquist. Trans. Caryl Emerson (Austin: University of Texas Press, 1982), 345.

2   In citing *St. Leon* but not pursuing the extensive thematic and plot correspondences with Frankenstein, recent studies follow Burton R. Pollin, "Philosophical and Literary Sources of *Frankenstein*," *Comparative Literature* 17 (1965): 97–108. See, for example, Chris Baldick, *In Frankenstein's Shadow* (Oxford: Clarendon Press, 1987), 37; Anne K. Mellor, *Mary Shelley: Her Life, Her Fiction, Her Monsters* (New York and London: Routledge reprint, 1989), 85; and Emily Sunstein, *Mary Shelley: Romance and Reality* (Baltimore: The Johns Hopkins UP, 1991, paperback edition), 23–24.

named above, the "strong precursor" with whom the "ephebe" grapples is not a poet of the past but a near contemporary. As the product of intertextual dialogue, Shelley's novel embodies the female child's quest for independence from patriarchal authority, but the act of asserting her independence is made problematic in this case by the fact that her "strong precursor" is not merely a near contemporary but her own father. Partially orphaned and then alienated by a stepmother whom she saw as a rival for her father's attention, Shelley's attachment to her father was perhaps also afflicted by a trace of culpability for her mother's death in childbirth.[3]

II.

Following Wollstonecraft's death in 1797, Godwin was left to care for their infant daughter and the three-year old Fanny Imlay. At this time he began to work on *St. Leon*, and the new novel, which anticipates the interest in history and the historical accuracy of his *Life of Chaucer* (1803) and *History of the Commonwealth of England* (1824–28), examines what Godwin described a few years before as "the evils which arise out of the present system of civilized society," and he considered the novel's publication an effort to "disengage the minds of men from prepossession, and launch them upon the sea of moral and political inquiry."[4] Thus *St. Leon* resumes the critique of "things as they are" that commenced with *An Enquiry Concerning Political Justice* (1793) and was continued in *Caleb Williams* (1794) and, like the previous novel, *St. Leon* was intended to make Godwin's political teachings more widely accessible. In particular, the new novel reveals the extent to which Godwin's views on marriage

---

3   Emily Sunstein takes a neutral stance in the dispute over the character of the second Mrs. Godwin as compared to the first and reminds the reader that Mary's singularly possessive attachment to her father was such that "no woman under Heaven, not even Mary Wollstonecraft had she descended from it, would have been readily accepted as her father's consort by the four-year-old Mary Godwin," *Mary Shelley: Romance and Reality*, 2.

4   *The British Critic* (July 1795), 95.

had been modified under the tutelage of Wollstonecraft; in fact, even friendly critics charged that he had recanted his revolutionary views on relationships between the sexes. (He concedes this point in the novel's Preface: "I apprehend domestic and private affections inseparable from the nature of man, and from what may be styled the culture of the heart, and am fully persuaded that they are not incompatible with a profound and active sense of justice in the mind that cherishes them.")[5] Scattered throughout the text, variations of this view contradict Godwin's memorable description of marriage given in Book VIII of *Political Justice* (1793) as "the worst of all monopolies."[6] And yet, the revised argument presented in *St. Leon*, which accommodates bourgeois family life, is but another example of the intertextual dialogue conducted between *Political Justice* and Godwin's prose fiction: the later texts suggest modifications to the ideology set down in the philosophical treatise.

The overall design and thematic patterns of *St. Leon* are replicated typologically in *Frankenstein*. At the center is a presentation of the "education" of the protagonist Reginald de St. Leon alternately via chivalry and alchemy. (Alchemy, it is implied, is analogous to chivalry; both are anachronistic social and scientific paradigms.) The latter is perceived initially by the protagonist as a possible vehicle by which he might simultaneously serve mankind and seek atonement for his betrayal of the chivalric code. Reginald's travels embody an ironic inversion of the classical *Bildungsreise*; his education is based on disillusioning rather than edifying experiences. And, anticipating the trajectory of the Monster's experience, rather than the popular gratitude he expects in response to his benevolent actions, suffering and destruction seem ineluctably to follow in his wake and he is rejected precisely by those whom he had intended

5   William Godwin, *St. Leon: A Tale of the Sixteenth Century*, 4 Volumes (London: Printed for G.G. & J. Robinson, R. Noble, printer, 1799), Vol. I, ix. Hereafter all intra-textual references are to this edition.

6   William Godwin, *An Enquiry Concerning Political Justice* (Third Edition, 1798), ed. Isaac Kramnick (Harmondsworth: Penguin Books, 1976), 762.

to help. As a result, he is hunted down by such adversaries as his son Charles and his erstwhile friend, Bethlem Gabor. Reginald's fate is shared by Victor and the Monster (who alternately serve as each other's prey), and parallels to all three characters are found in the tragic situation of Oedipus. Sophocles's tragedy, *St. Leon,* and *Frankenstein* are all myths of misguided benevolence in which hubristic transgression of social, religious, and epistemological boundaries is punished by exile from human society. Mary Godwin also suffers ostracism from her family following her elopement with Shelley—an intolerable act of rebellion against her father's authority—which coincides with a new phase of authorship independent of her father's influence. And yet her new status as an author connects her more closely than ever to her precursors Godwin, Wollstonecraft, and Shelley.

Following his disillusioning experience of the brutalities of war in the Italian campaigns of French King Francis I (1494–1547), Reginald finds himself ill-equipped to function in civilian society. Precisely because he is publicly celebrated as a paragon of chivalry who no longer believes in its values, Godwin presents his fall from grace as symptomatic of a culture in decline. Thus chivalry, Edmund Burke's shibboleth in *The Reflections on the Revolution in France* and Godwin's target in *Caleb Williams,* is exposed as already otiose even during its supposed heyday. A living anachronism driven to gambling, Reginald forfeits his family's honor and fortune. Flying from France in disgrace, he settles his family near Lake Geneva. The idyllic scene is reminiscent of the De Laceys' cottage in the forest where Victor's Monster finds refuge.

The appearance of a mysterious interloper, Zampieri, violates the intimacy of the family circle and awakens Reginald's dormant ambition. The stranger offers to share the mystery of the philosopher's stone and the *elixir vitae* but only on condition that Reginald agrees in advance not to share this secret with anyone, not even Marguerite, his high-minded wife. Her character is an idealized portrait of Mary Wollstonecraft and serves as the model for all the

noble female characters in *Frankenstein*: Caroline, Agatha, Safie, Jus-
tine, and Victor's cousin, childhood companion, and fiancée Elizabeth Lavenza. Reginald's first impulse is to refuse Zampieri's offer,
insisting that his "heart was formed by nature for social ties . . . and
I will not now consent to anything that shall infringe on the happiness of my soul." (II, 7) Zampieri responds by striking at Reginald's
Achilles' heel; as a true knight and the flower of French chivalry he
desires to serve once again as an agent of justice and public welfare:
"Feeble and effeminate mortal! Was ever a great discovery prose-
cuted, or an important benefit conferred upon the human race, by
him who was incapable of standing, and thinking, and feeling,
alone?" (II, 7, 8) The esoteric skills are imparted and immediately Reginald experiences a complete resurrection of his former pride and
ambition. His transformation parallels Victor's metamorphosis following the creation of his hideous offspring, but as the bearer of a
monstrous secret he embarks on an odyssey "hated by mankind,
hunted from the face of the earth, pursued by atrocious calumny,
without country, without a roof, without a friend." (II, 9)

While Reginald's and Victor's horrible inner transformation is
comparable, the knowledge engendering such change in the psyche
of the protagonists is different and must be distinguished. In contrast to the "new science" of natural philosophy that engenders Victor's creative act of hubris, Godwin's protagonist, Reginald de St.
Leon, pursues the arcane arts of alchemy, but both Reginald and Victor are both afflicted by a mania for illicit knowledge that Chris
Baldick has called "epistemophilia."[7] Knowledge *per se* is, however,
not the crucial issue; it is rather the specific character of the
knowledge that they seek. Awakened by the writings of Cornelius
Agrippa, Paracelsus, and Albertus Magnus, alchemy is also Victor's
first intellectual passion, and he confesses to Walton that "if only he
had been content to study the more rational theory of chemistry
which had resulted from modern discoveries" it is possible "that the

---

7   Baldick, *op. cit.*, 26.

train of my ideas would never have received the fatal impulse that led to my ruin." The following passage, with its self-analysis and confessional tone, might just as easily have been spoken by Godwin's protagonist:

> My dreams were therefore undisturbed by reality, and I entered with the greatest diligence into the search of the philosopher's stone and the elixir of life. But the latter obtained my most undivided attention: wealth was an inferior object, but what glory would attend the discovery, if I could banish disease from the human frame, and render men in vulnerable to any but a violent death.[8]

Masao Miyoshi observes that "in *Frankenstein* the main vehicle of Gothic fantasy is no longer the conventional supernatural" such as alchemy; instead, it is the "new science," which, as a result of the protagonist's misapplication, vitiated its claims to being "a humane pursuit by demonstrating its possible monstrous results." Shelley reveals in her appropriation and revision of her father's novel that "science," the definitive Enlightenment pursuit, "can generate a totally new species of terror. If scientific man is a kind of God, his scientific method becomes a new supernaturalism, a contemporary witchdoctoring of frightening potential."[9] But clearly, what Reginald and Victor have most in common is the abuse of their respective sciences. Both novels present the distortion and perversion of procreation as a misapplication of science, old and new, and the process leading to Mary Godwin's emergence as a novelist corresponds to Reginald's application of alchemy and Victor's exploitation of the "new science," since all three processes presuppose the transgression of nature, established authority, and, ultimately, the social order.

---

8   Mary Shelley, *Frankenstein: or, The Modern Prometheus* (1818 edition), in *The Mary Shelley Reader*, ed. Betty T. Bennett and Charles E. Robinson (New York: Oxford UP, 1990), 30. All intra-textual references are to this edition.
9   Masao Miyoshi, *The Divided Self: A Perspective on the Literature of the Victorians* (New York: New York UP, 1969), 86.

The enormous destructive potential of Reginald and Frankenstein's secret powers condemns them to the remorseless isolation
experienced by all those who possess the Midas touch, starting with
Godwin himself, whose influence as a philosopher appears under
the guise of alchemy and science in both novels.[10] If Reginald's
powers are shared with others the laws of nature will be violated,
thus posing a threat to the whole basis of human civilization: "Exhaustless wealth, if communicated to all men, would be but an exhaustless heap of pebbles and dust; and nature will not admit her
everlasting laws to be so abrogated, as they would be by rendering
the whole race of sublunary man immortal." (II, 103) In this way,
Reginald's concerns over the potential misuse of his powers anticipate Victor's principled refusal to create a female companion for the
Monster. It is important to note that altruism dominates the following passage and not, as Anne K. Mellor insists,[11] fear of female sex-
uality or the conscious drive to "usurp" the female principle in procreation:

> I was now about to form another being of whose dispositions I was alike
> ignorant; she might become ten thousand times more malignant than her
> mate and delight, for its own sake, in murder and wretchedness. He had
> sworn to quit the neighborhood of man and hide himself in deserts; but she
> had not; and she, who in all probability was to become a thinking and rea-
> soning animal, might refuse to comply with a compact made before her cre-
> ation . . . . Even if they were to leave Europe and inhabit the deserts of the
> new world, yet one of the first results of those sympathies for which the de-
> mon thirsted would be children, and a race of devils would be propagated

10 Gary Kelly is persuaded that Mary's father "felt himself to be in possession of
    great and terrible secrets: the philosophy of *Political Justice* which he could not
    use for the benefit of mankind, but which, on the contrary, made him an object
    of fear and loathing," *The English Jacobin Novel, 1780–1805* (Oxford: Oxford UP,
    1976), 209. Emily Sunstein (*op. cit.*, 20) notes that Godwin's contemporaries
    "compared him to a great, if failed explorer on humanity's behalf, a Promethean
    paradigm that Mary Godwin would immortalize in her scientist, Frankenstein,
    whose confidant, Walton, is a polar explorer" and would-be altruist savior of
    mankind.
11 "The Female in *Frankenstein,*" in *Feminism and Romanticism,* ed. Anne K. Mellor
    (Bloomington, Indiana: Indiana UP, 1988), 224.

upon the earth who might make the very existence of the species of man a condition precarious and full of terror. Had I a right for my own benefit, to inflict this curse upon everlasting generations? (122–123)

The use of his illicit powers increases Reginald's sense of isolation, and his lament resonates with his counterpart's in *Frankenstein*: "Man was not born to live alone. He is linked to his brethren by a thousand ties; and, when those ties are broken, he ceases from all genuine existence." (III, 97) But rather than put an end to his wretched wanderings, Reginald, after employing the *elixir vitae* in order to make good his escape from the Spanish Inquisition, "panted for something to contend with and something to conquer. My senses unfolded themselves to all the curiosity of remark; my thoughts seemed capable of industry unwearied, and investigation the most constant and invincible. Ambition revived in my bosom . . . desired to perform something . . . that I might see the world start at and applaud." (III, 284)

Illustrating Godwin's prowess in the historical travel mode made popular by Ann Radcliffe and M. G. Lewis, Reginald crosses Europe and finds his desired new field of action in Hungary. Ravaged by war, famine, and grinding servitude under the Turks, the inhabitants of this nation seem ready for a savior, and Reginald seizes the chance to atone for the death of his wife and the breakup of his family with some supreme act of charity and benevolence. However, rather than endearing himself to his Hungarian hosts, the gold he creates in order to buy wheat undermines the nation's markets, stokes runaway inflation, and increases the suffering of the population. Once again, the use of alchemy has been shown to disrupt the laws of nature and society and to alienate the protagonist still further from the human circle. Reginald's ostracism marks him as another member of the band of Romantic outcasts: the Ancient Mariner, Childe Harold, Prometheus, and his literary double, Victor Frankenstein. Transgression is the natural consequence of hubris, and it is punished by exile from one's home culture. Mary suffers ostracism from her family as a result of transgressing her father's will and the hubris of elopement is equated with the exercise of her procreative powers and her emergence as the author of her own literary texts. This is the same pattern of creation/transgression/isolation replicated in *St. Leon* and *Frankenstein*. Release from this condition is achieved only in confession or by acts of unselfish caring that lead to absolution. But such deliverance is denied to Reginald and Victor. Even though the Monster reads Victor's lab notes, his scientific method is never disclosed to others. Similarly, Reginald keeps his promise to Zampieri and the secret of the philosopher's stone is never revealed to the reader. Indeed, the entire first-person narrative in *St. Leon* forms a series of complex circumlocutions corresponding to the evasive actions and disguises that Reginald requires to preserve his secret at all costs. Instead of genuine communication, Godwin's protagonist offers what he admits is only the semblance of communication and "the unburdening of the mind" simply because he recognizes it is of the essence of being human "insatiably [to thirst] for a confident [sic] and a friend." (II, 103) Reginald's faux confession functions merely as auto-therapy, and his sufferings, while offering an admonition to the reader, are not redeemed. He is doomed to continue his wanderings without respite.

III.

Written by Mary when she was only nineteen, *Frankenstein* is among the most enduring icons of Romanticism, and in recent years it has attracted as much attention from critics as any text in the canon. As the only daughter of Godwin and Wollstonecraft's ill-fated union, Mary was "nursed and fed with a love of glory. To be something great and good was the precept given me by my father."[12] Emily Sunstein dismisses as inaccurate the assumption still accepted by some that Mary received no systematic education prior

---

12   *Journals of Mary Wollstonecraft Shelley*. Abinger MSS, 21 (October 1838).

to falling under the influence of Shelley. "Living with Godwin was an education; she loved leaning; he encouraged her, and gave her the background Wollstonecraft had not had and regretted having missed."[13] Years later, Jane (later Claire) Clairmont corroborated her stepsister's account of the tenor and routine of their Godwinian education:

> All the family worked hard, learning and studying: we all took the liveliest interest in the great questions of the day: common topics, gossiping, scandal, found no entrance in our circle, for we had been brought up by Mr. Godwin to think it was the greatest misfortune to be fond of the world, or worldly pleasures or of luxury or money; and that there was no greater happiness than to think well of those around us, and to delight in being useful or pleasing to them.[14]

Godwin described the spirit that governed Mary's education in this way: "I am anxious that she should be brought up like a philosopher even like a Cynic. It will add greatly to the strength and worth of her character."[15] Her father's choice of a second wife was only the first of devastating paternal rebuffs she suffered; the other was his reaction to her elopement with the older married poet, which may be seen as an effort to establish independence from Godwin's control over her discourse.[16] As the precocious child grew into a young woman and emerged as an author, her father's texts pro-

---

13 Emily Sunstein, *Mary Shelley: Romance and Reality*, 38–39: "All the children were deeply influenced by him, but Mary was his star disciple, the most powerfully engaged and permanently affected, the one from whom he demanded and gave most. Her most felicitous, intimate, even thrilling intercourse with her father was that of pupil and teacher, and most inordinate as her later tributes to him might seem, it was homage to mentorship that few fathers gave their daughters."

14 *Journals of Claire Clairmont*, ed. M.K. and D. M. Stocking (Cambridge, Mass.: Harvard UP, 1968), 18.

15 Letter to W.T. Baxter, 8 June 1812 in *Shelley and His Circle, 1773–1822*, ed. Keith Neil Cameron and Donald H. Reiman (Cambridge, Mass.: Harvard UP, 1961–73), 3, 102.

16 Evidence for Mary's idolization of her father is found in a letter: "Until I met Shelley, I may justly say that Godwin was my God," *The Letters of Mary Wollstonecraft Shelley*, ed. Betty T. Bennet (Baltimore: The Johns Hopkins UP, 1980), 1, 296.

vided the authoritative discourse with which she contended in an effort to establish her own distinctive voice. Her earliest literary efforts were, of course, published by the Juvenile Library, her stepmother's publishing venture, and Mellor suggests that there is "a peculiar symbolic resonance" in the loss of Mary's early writings which were "accidentally" left behind at a Parisian hotel: "Mary's first impulse in her new life with the poet Shelley was to establish her own literary credentials, to assert her own voice, and to assume a role as his intellectual companion and equal."[17] But at least initially she merely exchanged one male tutor for another; it was only with her emergence as an author that she attained liberation from both father and husband.

While a number of candidates for Mary's precursor text are named or cited in the novel, including those by Milton, Plutarch, and Goethe, *St. Leon* is the "adult" text for which *Frankenstein* serves as a reduction, translation, and revision. Its author combined the functions of Mary's father and mother as well as her chief teacher and her chief literary "precursor," and yet the most striking structural and thematic correspondences between *Frankenstein* and *St. Leon* arise from the urgency of Mary's efforts to mediate her Godwinian education by re-writing one of its canonical texts. In a modification of the Russian linguist I. M. Lotman's model of the "reception" and "appropriation" of adult texts by children, Michael Holquist suggests that "not only do children thus limit the scripts of the playlets their parents enact with them; they also limit the size of the cast. That is, for children all possible players in the world's drama are reduced to the characters experienced in the family culture."[18] Barbara Johnson has written that "*Frankenstein* can be read as the story of the experience of writing *Frankenstein*," but actually

---

17   Anne K. Mellor, *Mary Shelley: Her Life, Her Fiction, Her Monsters* (New York and London: Routledge, 1989), 23.

18   Michael Holquist, *Dialogism: Bakhtin and his World* (New York and London: Routledge, 1990), 82.

the writing of *Frankenstein* is about the re-writing of *St. Leon*.[19] This accounts for the parallels between *St. Leon* and *Frankenstein* with respect to their dramatic personae. The model for St. Leon's family is, of course, Godwin's own deceased first wife, daughters, and stepson; and in *Frankenstein* Mary sustains this pattern, less as a way of exorcising an Electra complex by gender substitution (in this sense Victor and Alphonse Frankenstein can be seen as surrogates for Shelley and Godwin; Elizabeth is Fanny Imlay's double) than as a means of completing her literary education. As such, education assumes the form, initially, of appropriating parental speech patterns and narratives. Once this step is successfully completed, the child moves on to the second stage in the process of *Bildung*: the articulation and creation of her own original discourse.

Bakhtin used the term "novel" to denote "whatever force is at work within a given literary system to reveal the limits and the artificial constraints of that system." According to this view, "literary systems are comprised of canons and novelization is fundamentally anticanonical."[20] This characterization applies to both *St. Leon* and *Frankenstein*, since each work is a militantly anti-canonical, composite literary form that explores the outer boundaries of the novel's possibilities as a genre and combines, appropriates, and fuses other narrative sub-genres, including the Gothic, travel, and sentimental fiction. Bakhtin argues that the content and images of the novel are therefore "profoundly double-voiced and double-languaged" because they "seek to objectivize the struggle with all types of internally persuasive discourse that had at one time held sway over the author."[21] One such sub-genre exhibited in *Frankenstein* that illustrates this process is the *Bildungsroman*, in which the process of intertextual dialogue has been fused with the dialectic of education.

---

19   Barbara Johnson, "My Monster/My Self," *Diacritics* 12 (1982): 8.
20   From the author's introduction, Mikhail Bakhtin, *The Dialogic Imagination: Four Essays*, xxxi.
21   Bakhtin, *op. cit.*, 348.

The composition of *Frankenstein* may, in fact, be compared to the manner in which children learn to appropriate adult speech for themselves and the means by which a writer distinguishes their voice from those of precursors and literary authority figures. The first process is analogous to translation in that it involves assimilation, rearrangement, a certain amount of necessary distortion, and simplification of the parental discourse adopted by the child as models in developing their own voice and speech patterns. Lotman describes language acquisition as a mediating process combining translation, appropriation, and reconfiguration:

> The child's contact with the world of adults is constantly imposed on him by the subordinated position of his world in the general hierarchy of the culture of adults. However, this contact itself is possible only as an act of translation. How can such translation be accomplished? . . . [T]he child establishes a correspondence between some texts familiar and comprehensible to him in "his" language and the texts of "adults" . . . . In such a translation — of one whole text by another whole text — the child discovers an extraordinary abundance of "superfluous" words in "adult" texts. The act of translation is accompanied by a semantic reduction of the text . . . . The child reduces the semantic model obtained from [the language of adults] in such a way that translation into his own language of the texts flowing from without is possible.[22]

The child's mediation of adult discourse thus may be likened to the reception of literary texts belonging to a foreign culture. In *Les voix du silence* (1951) André Malraux describes the process of cultural interaction in terms of a "conquest," an "annexation," a "possession" of the "foreign," of that which is culturally "other," and Bakhtin characterizes the impact of another's discourse upon the writer as a dialectical opposition between the self and the other involving, first, the recognition of difference that is then followed by the struggle for individuation or originality:

---

22   I.M. Lotman, "On the Reduction and Unfolding of Sign Systems," in *Semiotics and Structuralism: Readings from the Soviet Union*, ed. Henryk Baran (White Plains, NY: International Arts and Sciences Press, Inc., 1976), 302.

> When someone else's ideological discourse is internally persuasive for us and acknowledged by us, entirely different possibilities open up. Such discourse is of decisive significance in the evolution of an individual's consciousness: consciousness awakens to independent ideological life precisely in a world of alien discourses surrounding it, and from which it cannot initially separate itself .... One's own discourse is gradually and slowly wrought out of other's words that have been acknowledged and assimilated, and the boundaries are at first scarcely perceptible .... When such influences are laid bare, the half-concealed life lived by another's discourse is revealed within the new context of the given author. When an influence is deep and productive, there is no external imitation, no simple act of reproduction but rather a further creative development of another's discourse in a new context and under new conditions.[23]

In its mythical treatment of the necessity to struggle against even the most beloved presence in one's life, Mary Shelley's novel also reflects the centrality to Romanticism of Germaine de Staël's maxim: "Force of mind is developed only by attacking power."

The Monster's acquisition of speech, reading skills, and, most importantly, the capacity to generate texts symbolically, replicates Mary's education as a struggle with another's, more powerful discourse. Within her narrative this process approximates the Lotman/Bakhtin paradigm according to which the Monster learns, first, by appropriating the discourse of the De Lacey family and of the books he finds in the "leathern portmanteau": Milton, Plutarch, and Goethe, and, secondly, in articulating its own individuated discourse.[24] In the Godwin household the categories of parents and authors were conflated, and the circle of family friends included prominent literary and cultural figures who were familiar to the children.[25] Mary's, and by extension, the Monster's obsession with

---

23 Bakhtin, *op. cit.*, 345, 347.

24 All of these works figured prominently in Godwin's scheme of education for his children, but Goethe's *Werther* carried especially deep emotional resonance for the Godwin family because William was reading it at the time of Wollstonecraft's death.

25 Regular visitors to the Godwin household included William Wordsworth, Charles Lamb, S.T. Coleridge, William Hazlitt, Thomas Holcroft, Joseph Johnson, Samuel Rogers, John Flaxman, J.M.W. Turner, Maria Edgeworth, Helen Maria Williams, and Charlotte Smith.

language reflects their shared struggle to gain command of a medium in which to express their own thoughts in the midst of many authoritative models of discourse: "By degrees I made a discovery of still greater moment: I found that these people possessed a method of communicating their experience and feelings to one another by articulate sounds . . . . This was indeed a godlike science, and I ardently desired to become acquainted with it." (83) There is a remarkable parallel between the Monster's language acquisition through a process of eavesdropping on the De Laceys and the famous anecdote of Mary and the other Godwin children hiding behind the sofa in order to hear Coleridge's reading of the "The Rime of the Ancient Mariner." How many countless times was this scene replicated over the years during visits by Wordsworth, Lamb, and Holcroft? An interesting irony disclosed in the dialogic process is how the Monster acquires and demonstrates a command over language that far surpasses the eloquence of any other figure in the novel. Indeed, the source of his eventual domination of Victor is not his superhuman strength, but his greater rhetorical power. It is also an irony of literary history that in securing her authorial identity with the endurance of *Frankenstein* Mary surpassed the success enjoyed by *St. Leon*, her primary precursor text, which Byron considered superior to *Caleb Williams*. And while *Frankenstein* continues to generate countless literary and cinematic spinoffs at a dizzying rate, Godwin's novel, until recently, was only available in an antiquarian reprint.

A further instance of Mary's identification with the Monster is found in their similar responses to maternal deprivation. Victor and Reginald are also motherless, and for both this loss is exacerbated by the deaths of other loved ones. Anne Mellor has described *Frankenstein* as "an analysis of the failure of the family, the damage wrought when the mother—or a nurturant parental love—is absent."[26] This is also the central theme of *St. Leon*, which is, as already

---

26   Mellor, *op. cit.*, 39.

suggested, a transparent redaction of the Godwin family experience, and Mary's treatment of the orphan's agony of the Monster illustrates Sigmund Freud's view that "missing someone who is loved and longed for is the key to an understanding of anxiety."[27] John Bowlby, the English psychologist and biographer of Charles Darwin, modifies Freud's observations on grief and separation anxiety to suggest a possible cause of Mary's frequent bouts of anxiety during her many pregnancies:

> States of anxiety and depression that occur during adult years, and also psychopathic conditions, can, it is held, be linked in a systematic way to the states of anxiety, despair, and detachment . . . that are so readily engendered whenever a young child is separated for long from his mother figure, whenever he expects a separation, and when, as sometimes happens, he loses her altogether.[28]

By virtue of a kind of sorcery akin to alchemy, Mary and the Monster seem to have been formed by a hermaphroditic father, who combines both the male and female principles of generation and whose powers of multiplication correspond to the recondite powers of the philosopher's stone. As a descriptive term "hermaphroditic" is preferable to William Veeder's "androgyne," since androgyny refers only to proclivity or "sexual character," while hermaphroditism actually has reference to actual sexual nature or capacity.[29] Victor's ability to create life from inanimate matter and Reginald's multiple rebirths by means of the *elixir vitae* are methods of creating life that circumvent the female body but not the maternal principle. In a thinly veiled disguise for Godwin's relationship to Mary and her half-sister Fanny, Reginald outlives his wife and appropriates

27   Sigmund Freud, *Inhibitions, Symptoms and Anxiety* (1926) in *The Complete Psychological Works of Sigmund Freud* (London: The Hogarth Press, 1953–1974), Vol. XX, 136–137.

28   John Bowlby, *Attachment and Loss, Separation: Anxiety and Anger* (New York: Basic Books, 1973), Vol. II, 4–5.

29   William Veeder, *Mary Shelley and Frankenstein — The Fate of Androgyny* (Chicago: U of Chicago Press, 1986).

the maternal role in his relationship to his daughters. The life-giving powers exhibited by Victor and Reginald correspond to Mary's own birth in which the maternal principle was eliminated in Wollstonecraft's death. Through their traumatic births and status as orphans the Monster stands revealed as her fictive other.

The main narrative and thematic vehicle in both novels — the perversion or misuse of science, old and new — is, in fact, a distortion of procreation, and the bridge between alchemy and natural philosophy is the discovery of the means of creating or perpetuating life by a subtraction of the female principle from procreation. Ironically, the stain of mortality is removed from persons *not of woman born*. The elimination of the female principle in procreation invites Mary's critique of the monstrosity of neglectful parenting. Testifying to the power of environmental conditioning in childhood, which is a fundamental teaching in Godwin's *Political Justice*, both motherless protagonists reveal themselves to be neglectful parents in their own right. And Victor's feckless record as the "parent" of the offspring of his scientific labors is symbolic of the neglectful male parents in Mary's personal life — Godwin and Shelley, Victor rationalizes the abandonment of his child on grounds not usually associated with maternalism, that is, aesthetic criteria, insisting "that no mortal could support the horror of that countenance"; even a "mummy endued with animation could not be so hideous as that wretch." (43) There are strong parallels here to Godwin's "monstrous" behavior as a parent, for we know that he not only opposed Mary's decision to elope with Shelley, but he also refused to claim or identify the body of Fanny Godwin following her suicide on October 9, 1816. (Like her half-sister, this doubly orphaned young woman had, in her father's view, indelibly stained the family's honor.) The novel also provides subversive commentary on the egregious behavior of other parents in the Shelley circle: Percy, Claire Clairmont, Byron, and even Mary herself. Byron gained custody of his daughter Allegra only to have her placed in a convent where she died of neglect. The frenetic wanderlust (and the woeful traveling conditions they endured) of the Shelleys may be directly implicated in the deaths of their children Clara I (March 6, 1815), Clara II (September 24, 1818), and William on June 7, 1819. Perhaps of all acts the most reprehensible was Shelley's abandonment of Harriet and their children when he eloped with Mary. In what can only be reckoned a display of astonishing insensitivity, Percy and Mary were then married less than three weeks after Harriet, who was pregnant at the time, drowned herself in the Serpentine in Hyde Park. Considering this monstrous record of neglect, which clearly contravened the teachings of Godwin by which the Shelleys claimed to be fashioning their lives, the Chancery judgment delivered on March 17, 1817 denying Percy custody of his children with Harriet could have come as no surprise and, respecting the moral universe of both *St. Leon* and *Frankenstein,* was certainly justified.[30]

With the appropriation and rewriting of *St. Leon* Mary attains independence, as a creator of texts, from both her father and her husband. For her husband, she serves as an extension of her father; her elopement and marriage to Shelley represent efforts on his part to attain consanguinity with her father, his great idol, through the instrumentality of her mind and body. At the same time, it reflects Percy's attempt to usurp Godwin's role as Mary's primary educator and literary precursor. We can see this as an attempted exclusionary gesture whose objective is to assume control over her continuing development as a writer. In *Frankenstein* Mary therefore seeks to perform a double divestiture not only of parental influence, but also of authoritative discourse associated with both dominating literary figures in her life, her father and her husband. In this way the novel serves as a powerful reminder that literary texts function instrumentally. In Holquist's phrase, "they serve as a prosthesis of the mind. As such, they have a tutoring capacity that materially

---

30   See Chapter Six, "Deaths by Land and Sea," in Robert Gittings and Jo Manton, *Claire Clairmont and the Shelleys, 1798–1879* (Oxford: Oxford UP, 1992), 66–73.

effects change by getting from one stage of development to another," and in its dual capacity as an enabling device and as a necessary stage in the dialectic of education leading to the attainment
of a secure authorial identity, *Frankenstein* enacts for its author and
protagonists a dual process of soul and voice formation.[31] Emulating Reginald's and Victor's search for ideal companionship, empowering knowledge and opportunities for doing some action that
is "great and good," the Monster's odyssey begins with the discovery that he lives in a hostile world and that he has been rejected by
his "father" and denied the right to engender his own offspring. His
odyssey or *Bildungsreise* ends with the murderous inversion of
Godwinian altruism as he lashes out at Victor, destroying all those
with whom he enjoys emotional intimacy in order to render his condition identical to his own. The rebellion of the Monster, which pro-
ceeds from inarticulate rage to the discovery of speech and the art
of discourse, invites comparisons with Mary's efforts, first, to assimilate and, secondly, to overcome her father's authoritative discourse, a process which culminates in her marriage to Shelley and
the nearly simultaneous inception of her novel.

Recognizing that even the most persuasive interpretation may
fail to convince, I would hesitate to suggest that the genesis and development of Mary's novel is fully explained as the result of intertextual dialogue with Godwin's *St. Leon*. Neither would I reduce
the text's function to mapping her development as a writer. But, as
I have attempted to show, such an interpretation brings us closer to
the novel's textual and psychological matrices and it delineates the
central autotherapeutic function of writing. Moreover, by adopting
Bakhtin's dialogic framework we gain a more pronounced awareness of the struggle involved in moving beyond mere appropriation
of another's authoritative discourse to the production of discourse
that is distinctly one's own. In contrast to those critics who have
inserted *Frankenstein* into or extracted the novel from a patriarchal
tradition, the preceding discussion should make it is possible to

---

31   Holquist, *op. cit.*, p. 83.

reject both alternatives. The tradition into which we should place *Frankenstein* is that which makes apparent its structure and language as empowering psychological scaffolding. Godwin's *St. Leon* provided Mary with a dialogic partner in the struggle for self-expression, and *Frankenstein* is a reflection of the will to articulate her own consciousness and to attain individuation apart from the discourse associated with the "strong precursors" in her personal and literary experience. What makes the intertextual dialogue forming *Frankenstein* of particular interest is that the authoritative discourse with which its young author contended was formed by the texts of her father, mother, and husband—a body of texts that she habitually and even ritually read at home and on her mother's grave in the St. Pancras churchyard. This is the tradition formed by *St. Leon*. From this perspective Mary's novel can be seen to replicate intertextual dialogue with a text that we can readily identify, *St. Leon,* and because of Shelley's filial relationship with its author, it is possible to extrapolate from this process of intertextual dialogue to her development and growth as a writer. The end result of this process is the acquisition and exercise of genuine cultural power.

3 Tolstoy and the "Spiritual Delights" of Schopenhauer

In a letter to the lyrical poet Afanasy Fet (1820–1892) written on August 30, 1869, Lev Tolstoy waxes ebullient over his discovery of the writings of Arthur Schopenhauer (1788–1860):

> Do you know what this summer has meant to me? Constant raptures over Schopenhauer and a whole series of spiritual delights which I've never experienced before. I've sent for all of his works and I'm reading them (I've also read Kant), and probably no student ever studied so much for his course, and learned so much, as I did this summer. I don't know if I'll ever change my opinion, but at present I'm certain that Schopenhauer is the most brilliant of men. I've begun to translate him and won't you also take it on? We could publish it jointly. As I read him, it's inconceivable to me how his name can remain *unknown* . . .[1]

It would be easy to dismiss this enthusiasm and the opinion it engendered as just another example Tolstoy's penchant for hyperbole. One could similarly ascribe this sentiment to the fleeting, but intense passion Tolstoy experienced in his encounter with the German philosopher and his major work, *Die Welt als Wille und Vorstellung* [*The World as Will and Representation*] (1819, 1844), which was strong enough momentarily to becloud the Russian novelist's judgment. But neither, in fact, is the case. Tolstoy's infatuation with Schopenhauer was neither exaggerated nor ephemeral. On the contrary, we see from Tolstoy's prose fiction and letters alike, that Schopenhauer's influence on Tolstoy was profound, pervasive, and, like the impact Schopenhauer exerted on Nietzsche, lifelong. Of course, the important role that Schopenhauer's thought played in the development of Tolstoy's artistic, ethical, and religious *Weltanschauung* is acknowledged in passing by leading critics of Tolstoy, from Henri Troyat and R. F. Christian to John Bayley and Theodore

---

1   R.F. Christian, ed. *Tolstoy's Letters, 1828–1879* (London: Athlone Press, 1978), Vol. I, 221.

Redpath. Few critics, however, have sounded the depths of Tolstoy's affinity for Schopenhauer's teachings on the "will" and even fewer have systematically traced the Schopenhauerian features of Tolstoy's art and thought. While limitations of space prevent a thorough examination of these problems at this time, the aim of this essay is to offer some basic insights into this formative relationship.

No other philosopher in the nineteenth century assigned such an integral role for art in the workings of his metaphysical system than Schopenhauer. Unlike many of his predecessors and contemporaries, such as Immanuel Kant (1724–1804), J.C. Fichte (1762–1814), and G.W.F. Hegel (1770–1831), Schopenhauer does not consider art merely an intellectual narcotic or, even worse, a frivolous deviation from the path of serious philosophical investigation. On the contrary, Schopenhauer accords to art and the artistic genius the highest distinction. For unlike the scientist, who is concerned with observing the phenomenal world and establishing laws for its behavior, the artist, whether his tools are paint and brush, blueprint and plumb, pen and paper, or string and bow, pursues higher, eternal truths. Accordingly, "every work of art really endeavors to show us life and things as they really are; but these cannot be grasped directly by everyone through the mist of objective and subjective contingencies. Art takes away this mist."[2] And, the mist cleared, the observer is momentarily relieved of his attachment to the will and is free to contemplate his relation to the world as will as a disinterested, will-less subject of knowledge.

If, among Kant's disciples and immediate heirs, F.W.J. Schelling (1775–1854), a contemporary and friend of the Schlegel brothers, Novalis, and Ludwig Tieck, consistently made the most far-reaching claims for the transcendental possibilities of artistic contemplation, Schopenhauer's seductively elegant style and central doctrine that escape from the tyranny of the will-driven life is possible by means of

---

2   Arthur Schopenhauer, *The World as Will and Representation*, 2 Volumes, trans. E.F.J. Payne (New York: Dover, 1966), II, 407. All intra-textual references are to this edition.

either artistic creation or aesthetic perception exercised far greater influence among philosophers and practicing artists. Starting in the 1890s, widespread disenchantment with "professional" systems of thought, such as Hegel's, led to an embrace of Friedrich Nietzsche and Schopenhauer's ideas. Intense enthusiasm for Schopenhauer also coincided with the rise of other aesthetic, pessimistic, and anti-rationalist credos. Some well-known examples include Richard Wagner's dramatization of what he mistakenly believed was Schopenhauer's "metaphysics of sexual love" in the opera *Tristan und Isolde* (1865) and Thomas Hardy's conflation of Schopenhauer's "will" and Hegel's "world historical individual" in *The Dynasts* (1904, 1906, 1908).

Besides Nietzsche, Wagner, and Hardy, a short list of Schopenhauer's admirers in those years could serve as a reliable guide to the dominant figures in the chief cultural centers of Europe, from London and Paris to Vienna and St. Petersburg—George Eliot, Gustave Flaubert, Émile Zola, Franz Kafka, Sigmund Freud, August Strindberg, Ivan Turgenev, and Lev Tolstoy. In fact, veneration for Schopenhauer is one of the features which otherwise dissimilar minds of European culture have in common, from proponents of Naturalism and Symbolism, from *The Birth of Tragedy* to *The Interpretation of Dreams*. Schopenhauer's impact upon the 1890s and the early years of the twentieth century is such that it is difficult to imagine the shape of early modernism without him, especially in such areas as music, philosophy, aesthetics, and psychology.

At this point, before moving forward with a discussion of Tolstoy's affinity for Schopenhauer, it might be useful first to offer a description of Schopenhauer's doctrine of "disinterested" contemplation, that is, the manner in which a will-less subject of knowing must necessarily behold a work of art or an object in nature. Never does Schopenhauer, in proclaiming the virtues of disinterested contemplation, have in mind the same kind of disinterestedness that Kant insists is essential in making aesthetic judgments. And yet, when Schopenhauer speaks of the withdrawal of the will and the submergence of individuality as being essential to the realization of aesthetic experience, it is clear that his starting point is Kant's foundational idea. At the same time, it would be incorrect to treat Schopenhauer's adaptation of Kant's teaching on disinterestedness as merely a kind of restatement of the Kantian position in Romantic terms. While in *The Critique of Judgment* Kant is chiefly interested in determining the status of aesthetic judgments and of eliciting their basis or ground in order to draw a sharp dividing line between aesthetic awareness and our ordinary or scientific knowledge of empirical facts, Schopenhauer, in a manner that is typically Romantic in orientation, argues that aesthetic awareness constitutes knowledge affording insight into reality of a higher order than that available through scientific inquiry. Similarly, Percy Bysshe Shelley (1792–1822), a nearly exact contemporary, in the year before his death, ascribes to poetry a power that

> awakens and enlarges the mind itself by rendering it the receptacle of a thousand unapprehended combinations of thought. Poetry lifts the veil from the hidden beauty of the world, and makes familiar objects be as if they were not familiar . . . . The great secret of morals is love; or a going out of our own nature, and an identification of ourselves with the beautiful which exists in thought, action, or person, not our own. A man, to be greatly good, must imagine intensely and comprehensively . . . . The great instrument of moral good is the imagination . . . . Poetry strengthens the faculty which is the organ of the moral nature of man . . .[3]

Schopenhauer gives the notion of disinterested contemplation a wider significance than that granted to it by Kant, so that it encompasses not only beauty, but also what Schopenhauer identifies as "the sublime." The nature of purely objective perception is such that it admits not only those objects which "accommodate themselves" to it, "when by their manifold and at the same time definite and distinct form they easily become representatives of their Ideas, in which beauty, in the objective sense consists," but also things positively "unfavorable to the will." (I, 205) Schopenhauer explains that the sensations evoked by the sublime are identical to the feelings associated with the contemplation of the beautiful, of the

---

3   Percy Bysshe Shelley, *A Defence of Poetry* (1822).

experience of pure will-less knowing, and knowledge of the eternal Ideas. "The feeling of the sublime is distinguished from that of the beautiful," only by the addition, "namely the exaltation beyond the known hostile relation of the contemplated object to the will in general." (I, 204–205) The feeling of the sublime varies according to the degree of danger that the beheld scene poses to the will:

> of the spectator. It is at its weakest when we behold a stark winter landscape and strongest when we are abroad in the storm of tempestuous seas . . . . [I]n the unmoved beholder of this scene the twofold nature of his consciousness reaches the highest distinctness. Simultaneously, he feels himself as individual, as the feeble phenomenon of the will, which the slightest touch of these forces can annihilate, helpless against powerful nature, dependent, abandoned to chance, a vanishing nothing in the face of stupendous forces; and he also feels himself as the eternal, serene subject of knowing, who as the condition of every object is the supporter of this whole world, the fearful struggle of nature being only his mental picture or representation . . . . This is the full impression of the sublime. (I, 207–208)

In a famous scene in Chapter 14 of *War and Peace* Tolstoy illustrates the experience of the sublime that is just as forceful as Schopenhauer's, even if it lacks his terrifying mystery:

> High up in the light sky hung the full moon. Forests and fields beyond the camp, unseen before, were now visible in the distance. And farther still, beyond those forests and fields, the bright, oscillating, limitless distance lured one to itself. Pierre glanced up at the sky and the twinkling stars in its far-away depths. "And all that is me, all that is within me, and it is all I!" thought Pierre.

The last sentence is nearly a verbatim extract from Schopenhauer: *tat twam asi*—"This is you"—his borrowing from the Upanishads—the recognition that there is no difference between I and Thou, or between the subject of pure will-less knowing and the contemplated world of phenomena. This is the pantheistic epiphany that Pierre experiences in the moonlight.

     To see through the *principium individuationis* [the distinction of one object or being from all others], to divine its illusory, truth-shrouding character; to experience the emotional intuition that the will is the same in the one and the all: this is the knowledge that lies at the heart of Schopenhauer's ethics—knowledge that is obtained primarily through aesthetic contemplation. Similarly, only in the aesthetic state, reached through purely objective contemplation, is it possible to attain knowledge of the *Ding-an-sich*, "the thing-in-itself," the foundation of reality, which Schopenhauer asserts is the will. The will is the ultimate, irreducible primeval principle of being, the source of all phenomena, the begetter present and active in every single one of them, the impelling force engendering the whole visible world and all life—for it is the will to live. It is this through and through; so that whoever says "will" is speaking of the will to live, and if you use the longer term you are guilty of a pleonasm. The will always desires but one thing: life, and more life. And why? Because the will finds life priceless? Because the will affords the experience of any objective knowledge of life? Of course not. All knowledge alike is foreign to the will; it is something independent of knowledge, it is entirely original and absolute, a blind urge, a fundamentally uncaused, utterly unmotivated force; so far from depending on any evaluation of life,[1] the converse is the case, and all judgments are dependent upon the strength of the will to live.

The will, then, this "in-itself-ness" of things, existing outside of time, space, and causality, blind and causeless, greedily, wildly, ruthlessly demands life, demands objectification, and this objectification occurs in such a way that its original unity became a multiplicity—a process that receives the appropriate name of the *principium individuationis*. The will, avid of life, to wreak its desire objectifies itself into the myriad parts of the phenomenal world existing in time and space; but simultaneously, the will remains in full strength in each single and smallest of those parts. The world, then, is the product and the expression of the will, the objectification of the will in space and time. But the world is at the same time something else besides: it is the *idea*, my representation, mine and yours, the idea of each one and each one's idea about himself—by virtue, that is, of the discerning mind, which the will created to be a light to it in the higher stages of its objectification, namely, the higher primates and human beings. Thus, in the upper stages of its individuation, even in animals and especially in humans, the highest and most complicated of all creatures, the will, to give itself aid, comfort, enlightenment, and security, kindles the light of the intellect which should make an idea or representation of the world—a kind of three-dimensional projection map of phenomena. It is noteworthy that, for Schopenhauer, it was not the intellect that brought forth the will; the converse was actually the case, the will brought forth the intellect. It is not intellect, mind, knowledge, that is the primary and dominant factor in experience; it is the will that dominates, and the intellect serves it. In a world entirely the work of the will, of absolute, unmotivated, causeless, and unvaluated life-urge, intellect occupies, of course, only second place.

Will, as the opposite pole of passive satisfaction, is naturally a condition of perpetual unhappiness; it is unrest, a striving for *something* that never leads to satisfaction or fulfillment—it is want, craving, avidity, demand, and ceaseless suffering; and a world or will can be nothing else but a world of suffering. As a writer ceaselessly tormented by insatiable passions and by the knowledge of humankind's irremediable sinfulness, Tolstoy concurred with Schopenhauer in the view that the ever striving will ought to enjoy the ascendant position over the intellect. Tolstoy's much vaunted notion of the "natural man" has at its root precisely this knowledge of the will's primacy over the intellect, of the superiority of humanity's savage instincts over the civilizing urge. And Tolstoy found an antidote to his own miseries and hope for the redemption of humankind in Schopenhauer's prescription of art and Christian, quietistic oblivion as the only means to achieve victory over the will. Art, or rather the contemplation of a work of art, has the power to free the intellect from its original subservience to the will, so that it rises above the trammels of everyday existence and beyond the illusory and only temporary satisfactions granted by the world of appearances. By the power of the artistic genius, whose talent consists in perceiving "not individual things which have their existence only in the relation, but the Ideas of such things," the mist is cleared. The "veil of Maya" is torn back and the inner meaning of reality is revealed in the eternal Ideas, existing outside space and beyond time. Thus, as Nietzsche writes, "the heroism of truth consists in ceasing one day to be time's plaything. In becoming, all is hollow, deceptive, superficial and contemptible; the riddle which man is to solve can only be solved in the unchangeable, in being, in being such-and-no-other."[4] At this point, the subject ceases to be merely individual and becomes the pure will-less subject of knowledge, the "clear eye" and "mirror of the inner nature of the world":

> Raised up by the power of the mind, we relinquish the ordinary way of considering things, and cease to follow under the guidance of the forms of the principle of sufficient reason merely their relations to one another, whose final goal is always the relation to our will . . . . We lose ourselves entirely in the object of contemplation . . . . We forget our individuality, our will, and continue to exist only as pure subject, as clear mirror of the object, so that it is as though the object alone existed without anyone to perceive it . . . (I, 178)

In the process of gaining such singular enlightenment one arrives simultaneously at the painless state, prized by Epicurus as the highest good and as the enviable condition of the gods; for the moment one is delivered from the miserable pressure of the will: "We celebrate the Sabbath of the penal servitude of willing; the wheel of Ixion stands still." (I, 196) Not only does artistic contemplation yield insight into the immutable and highest truths of existence, it also provides emancipation from the tyranny of the will. The creative state, however, a sojourn among images irradiated by the Ideas, does not bring the final redemption. According to Schopenhauer, the aesthetic condition is but the prior stage to a perfected one in which the will, not permanently satisfied in the aesthetic, would be once for all outshone by knowledge, and would be annihilated. The consummation of the artist is the saint, who recognizes, in Samuel Johnson's phrase, the "vanity of human wishes," and, by acts of

---

4   Friedrich Nietzsche, *Schopenhauer as Educator*, trans. James W. Hillesheim and Malcom R. Simpson (Southbend, Indiana: Regnery/Gateway, 1965), 47.

self-abnegation, has the capacity to deny the will-to-live. Liberated from subservience to the will, knowledge then becomes pure perception, pure objectivity, pure repose. In Nietzsche's words, "Schopenhauerian man" is he who "voluntarily takes the pain of truthfulness upon himself, and this suffering serves to kill his individual will to prepare for that complete revolution and reversal of his being, the attainment of which is the actual meaning of life."[5]

By making such large claims for aesthetic experience (the contemplation of a work of art), Schopenhauer's philosophy is naturally the artist's philosophy *par excellence*. And Schopenhauer has, from the mid-nineteenth century onwards, found among artists and the initiated in the arts his most enthusiastic admirers and most fanatical converts. From Tolstoy's remarks to Fet, it is clear that the novelist heard more than just a sympathetic voice in the teaching of Schopenhauer, but that he also experienced the most illuminating, productive, and stimulating intellectual encounter he had ever had, nothing more and nothing less than a revelation. In Schopenhauer's teaching of the will, Tolstoy received an acceptable answer to the questions that he in his despair had addressed to the universal void: "Only put 'the service of God,'" he told Fet, "in place of 'the recognition of the vanity of life,' and we agree." For Tolstoy,

> never had anyone written anything more profound or true about the sufferings of man, struggling with all his "will to live" against the forces of destruction or about chastity, the negation of the species, as the means to perfect happiness. Ah, the bitter vigor of this Teuton, his savage pessimism, his aspirations to oriental serenity.[6]

Nietzsche, whose lifespan (1844–1900) fits neatly within Tolstoy's own (1828–1910) and whose mission it was to bring art and knowledge, science and passion, even nearer to each other, to make truth and beauty mingle together, even more tragically and

---

5   Nietzsche, *Schopenhauer as Educator*, 43.
6   Letter to Fet dated 30 August 1969 in *Tolstoy's Letters, 1828–1879*, ed. R.F. Christian (London: Athlone Press, 1978), Vol. I, 221.

thrillingly than Schopenhauer before him, makes an observation in the third part of his *Thoughts out of Season: Schopenhauer as Educator* that has particular relevance for Tolstoy's interest in and utilization of Schopenhauer's thought:

> Your true educators and molders disclose the true original meaning and the basic material of your being, which is something quite incapable of being educated or molded . . . . Your educators can be nothing more than your liberators . . . Education is . . . a rooting out of all weeds, rubbish and vermin from around the buds of the plants, a radiation or light and warmth, a loving, whispering fall of night rain; it is the imitation and adoration of nature in her motherly and compassionate mood; it is the consummation of nature.[7]

In later years, even after both Nietzsche and Tolstoy had renounced Schopenhauer as their guide, neither ceased to love what they had nonetheless ceased to believe. One may even say that after Nietzsche and Tolstoy had consciously stopped moving in Schopenhauerian trains of thought, their subsequent work was nonetheless a continuation and interpretation of Schopenhauer's world-picture instead of an actual departure from it. Indeed, to the end of his life, Tolstoy's library at Yasnaya Polyana was decorated by portraits of Dickens, Fet, and, Schopenhauer.

The basis for Tolstoy's allegiance to Schopenhauer was the possibility the German offered of arriving at highly moral results from highly sensual and passionate experimental premises. Tolstoy deduced from Schopenhauer's teachings on the illusory nature of life a congenial doctrine whose leading elements consisted of compassion, redemption, and self-abnegation. Dissolving the divisions between me and them parts the "veil of Maya" thereby disclosing ultimate reality. What was most appealing to Tolstoy about this doctrine is suggested by Schopenhauer himself: "The moral result of Christianity, up to the most exalted asceticism, finds [itself] in my work rationally based . . . whereas in Christianity they are based in

---

7   Nietzsche, *Schopenhauer as Educator*, 6.

sheer fables. Faith in these disappears more and more; thus people will be forced to turn to my philosophy." (II, 463) The central concerns of Schopenhauer's philosophy are sex, death, and history.[8] And Tolstoy's treatment of these substantive matters in his two major novels bears the imprint of Schopenhauer's meditations on the will.

Schopenhauer, in the supplementary essay, "On Death and Its Relation to the Indestructibility of Our Inner Nature," writes that "death is the real inspiring genius of philosophy, and for this reason Socrates defined philosophy as 'preparation for death.' Indeed, without death there would hardly have been any philosophizing." (II, 463) In *War and Peace* (1869) the rhythm of detached, journalistic description of battles, counterbalanced by charming details of domestic life, is broken only when the narrator provides philosophical commentary or in scenes into which death intrudes. The literary historian John Bayley concurs: "Where death is concerned, Tolstoy in *War and Peace* was under the spell of Schopenhauer. Life is a sleep and death an awakening: 'An awakening from life came to Prince Andrei together with his awakening from sleep. And compared to the duration of life it did not seem to him slower than an awakening from sleep compared to the duration of a dream.'"[9] Indeed, the second sentence comes almost verbatim from *The World as Will and Representation*. For Schopenhauer, death is an awakening from the feverish dreams of which life is composed: "they are the dreams that Hamlet asks about in the famous monologue." (II, 469) Prince Andrei's peaceful demeanor on the field of Austerlitz and his deathbed composure following the evacuation of Moscow are possible because of his recognition of death as the onset of "that liberation from the one-sidedness of an individuality which does not constitute the innermost kernel of our true being, but it is rather to

8   See R.F. Christian's discussion of the source of the biblical epigraph to *Anna Karenina* ("Vengeance is mine and I will repay"), which "Tolstoy originally borrowed from Schopenhauer," in *Tolstoy: A Critical Introduction* (Cambridge: Cambridge UP, 1969), 171–173.

9   John Bayley, *Tolstoy and the Novel* (London: Chatto and Windus, 1966), 82.

be thought of as a kind of aberration thereof. True freedom again enters at this moment which in the sense stated can be regarded as a *restitutio in integrum* [restoration of the original condition of oneness]." (II, 508) In other words, Prince Andrei realizes that while "death is the violent destruction . . . of the fundamental error of our true nature . . . . [T]here is something in us that death cannot destroy." (II, 507, 490) His peaceful countenance and quiet reflections seem to say, "I shall always be" and "always been." Accordingly,

> with death consciousness is certainly lost, but not with what produced and maintained consciousness; life is extinguished, but with it not the principle of life which manifested itself in it. Therefore, a sure and certain feeling says to everyone that there is in him something positively imperishable and indestructible. (II, 496)

Prince's Andrei's epiphany becomes the template for the conversion experiences of other Tolstoyan protagonists, such as Ivan Illych, who is granted enlightenment just before his painful death, and Konstantin Levin (in *Anna Karenina*) who undergoes a remarkable transformation as he witnesses the slow, agonizing death of his beloved brother. The approach of death acts as the catalyst for Levin's self-renewal. He is resolved to improve his life and to make amends for past sins:

> Death, the inevitable end of everything, confronted him for the first time with irresistible force. And death, which was close to his beloved brother, who was moaning in his sleep and by habit calling indiscriminately both on God and the devil, was not so far away as it had hitherto seemed to him. It was in himself too he felt it. If not today, then tomorrow, if not tomorrow, then thirty years hence—what difference did it make? And what this inevitable death was, he not only did not know, he not only never thought of it, but could not and dared not think of it. "I'm working, I want to do something but I had forgotten that it will all come to an end, that it will end in death . . ."

Just when the question of how to live had become a little clearer to him, he was confronted by a new, insoluble problem, that of death. Levin's despair at his brother's death is intensified by the ego-crushing realization of the futility of his individual efforts and the vanity of his personal ambition in the face of the total annihilation of his individuated self by death. He realizes all-too-painfully that his attempts to get at the heart of things are vain, for what he and Schopenhauer are concerned with knowing lies beyond time and space, and beyond, moreover, the phenomenal representation that shrouds the *Ding-an-sich*, and God, from sight. As Patrick Gardiner explains,

> ethics is mysterious, at least in so far as it remains opaque to normal modes of rational comprehension. One is reminded of some of Levin's reflections at the end of *Anna Karenina* concerning the moral vision that cannot be explained or dissected by "reason," since it pertains to what lies beyond "the chain of cause and effect," beyond the scope of concepts like consequence and reward.[10]

Tolstoy's awareness of the futility of ethical meditation and the acts of individual human beings is itself a major — if not *the* major — protagonist of *War and Peace.* According to Bayley,

> as in Schopenhauer, whom Tolstoy so much admired, the individual will goes for very little. Men are as helpless at parties as generals are on the battlefield. Pierre may continue to seek, to look for meanings and to find them, but he is really preempted by the fatalism of the plot, which controls the actions of individuals and nations, and determines that everything happens as it has to happen . . .[11]

Try as one may to come to an understanding of the laws of history out of the flux of human actions and motivations, one's comprehension of the order of things "must be followed as a matter of course by the thought that this order is only a superficial phenomenon, that such a constant arising and passing away cannot in any way touch the root of things, but can be relative, indeed only apparent." Further, for Schopenhauer, "the true inner being of everything, which, moreover, evades our glance everywhere and is thoroughly mysterious, is not affected by that arising and passing away, but rather continues to exist undisturbed thereby." Whatever sense one

---

10   Patrick Gardiner, *Schopenhauer* (Baltimore: Penguin Books, 1963), 277–278.
11   Bayley, *Tolstoy and the Novel*, 105.

makes of the destiny of humankind or the higher schemes of Providence "can never be the true order of things, but rather a mere veil covering an order, or more correctly a phenomenon conditioned by the constitution of our intellect." (II, 474) Like Schopenhauer, Tolstoy saw that time and space defeat one's ability to see beneath the ever-changing surface of phenomena to the realm of permanent Ideas, which stands "like a rainbow on the waterfall." As a consequence, human beings are unaware of the fact that "everything is always there and in its place, just as if everything were imperishable." Again, to quote a passage from *The World as Will and Representation*—which may have served as a model and inspiration for Tolstoy's historical and metaphysical speculations in the epilogue to *War and Peace*—in beholding nature one sees that the plant always flourishes and blooms, the insect hums, animal and

> human beings are there in evergreen youth, and every summer we again
> have before us the cherries that have already been a thousand times enjoyed.
> Nations also exist as immortal individuals, though sometimes they change
> their names. Even their actions, what they do and suffer, are always the
> same, though history pretends to relate something different; for it is like the
> kaleidoscope, that shows us a new configuration at every turn, whereas re-
> ally we always have the same thing before our eyes. (II, 478)

The thematic framework of *War and Peace* is thoroughly Schopenhauerian: as long as one does not deny the will one is helpless and cannot alter the course of history, let alone one's own personal destiny. Instead, one is forced to suffer perpetually "the penal servitude of willing" and to repeat the fundamental error of existence. That is, to go on living in ignorance of the blind force that impels both man's pettiest and noblest efforts: the will to live.

4 Rilke's Self-Portrait and the Example of Rodin

"You must work, always work."

Rodin to Rilke

The *Neue Gedichte* (*New Poems*) emerged from the period of Rainer Maria Rilke's close association with the French sculptor Auguste Rodin (1840–1917) in 1907. The origin of the radically new concept of poetry embodied in the two volumes of the *New Poems* is to be found in the artistic metamorphosis of Rilke from the kind of poet who lives according to the dictates of inspiration to the artisan poet-master of self and reality for whom work, daily labor and painstaking observation, is its own inspiration and its own reward.

In a letter of August 8, 1903 Rilke writes to Lou Andreas-Salomé (1861–1937) of his first visit to Rodin's studio. From the very first moment Rilke felt in awe of a personality so vast and self-sufficient that it bore within itself the security, comforts, and peace of a house and forest preserve:

> wußte ich, daß sein Haus nichts für ihn war, eine kleine armselige Notdurft vielleicht, ein Dach für Regen- und Schlafzeit; und daß es keine Sorge War für ihn und an seiner Einsamkeit und Sammlung kein Gewicht. Tief in sich trug er eines Hauses Dunkel, Zuflucht und Ruhe, und darüber war er selbst Himmel geworden und Wald herum und Weite und großer Strom, der immer vorüberfloß.[1]

Rodin's serene inwardness in the midst of the great city of Paris, his disciplined aloofness from superficiality, his patient observation, and his tireless receptivity to human beings, natural phenomena, and inanimate objects alike, made a profound impression on the

---

1   "I knew that his house meant nothing to him, a small paltry necessity, perhaps, a roof for time of rain and sleep; and that it was no concern to him and no burden upon his solitude and composure. Deep inside himself he carried the darkness, refuge, and quiet of a house, and he himself had become a sky above it, and forest around it, and a great stream continuously flowing by."

61

young poet. From his observations of Rodin's working methods Rilke learned to see "Dinge . . . in allem" [things in the midst of all], to seek his own "die Möglichkeit: Dinge zu bauen" [opportunity to construct things], to know "daß auch in Auf und Ab einer ruhigen Flasche Bewegung ist" [that even in the rise and fall of a quiet surface there is movement], which defines forms "genau und deutlich" [precisely and clearly]. But even more important for Rilke's subsequent development as a poet was the compelling example of the methodical workmanship of Rodin in plaster, marble, and bronze. Rilke perceived that Rodin's art was the product of "Handwerk" [craft] and bore the marks of daily labor and unremitting effort— "aus dem fast absichtslosen und demütigen Willen, immer bessere Dinge zu machen" [from the almost unintentional and humble desire to create better and better things]. Rilke envied and strove to emulate the discipline and hard-won mastery over self and materials which are reflected in Rodin's art; an art, as Rilke observes, that

> konnte nur von einem Arbeiter ausgehen, und der es gebaut hat, kann ruhig die Inspiration leugnen; sie kommt nicht über ihn, weil sie im ihm ist, Tag und Nacht, verursacht von jedem Schauen, eine von jeder Bewegung seiner Hand erzeugte Warme.[2]

In following Rodin's example, Rilke confesses to Andreas-Salomé that he must follow him

> nicht in einem bildhauerischen Umgestalten, meines Schaffens,aber in der inneren Anordhung des kunstlerischen Prozesses; nicht bilden muß ich lernen von ihm, aber tiefes Gesammeltsein um des Bildens willen. Arbeiten muß lernen, arbeiten, Lou, das fehlt mir so![3]

---

2   Also, from the letter of August 8, 1903 to Salomé: "Could only have been produced by a Worker, and he who had built it can quietly ignore inspiration; inspiration doesn't come over him because it is actually in him, day and night, awakened by each act of observation, a warmth engendered by every movement of his hand."

3   "Not in a sculptural transformation of my creative work, but in the inner reorganization of the artistic process; I must learn from him not how to work but

Rilke sought to make out of labor and craftsman-like diligence a bulwark against the ebb and flow of daily events, against the flux of time, which hitherto had taxed his powers of discrimination and robbed him of the serenity necessary for creative receptivity.

Sustained concentration and continuous movement, finely tooled detail, detached observation, an organic relation of parts to the whole, and linguistic innovation characterize the best of the *Neue Gedichte*. A passage from Rilke's letter of August 8th could serve as a shorthand index of the kinds of subjects that lent themselves to such rigorous examination and experiments in representation:

> Nur die Dinge reden zu mir. Rodins Dinge, die Dinge an den gotischen Kathedralen, die antikischen Dinge,—all Dinge, die vollkommene Dinge sind . . . . Ich fange an Neues zu sehen: schon sind mir Blumen oft so unendlich viel, und aus Tieren kamen mir Anregungen seltsamer Art. Und auch Menschen erfahre ich schon manchmal so, Hände leben irgendwo, Munde reden, und ich schaue alles ruhiger und mit größerer Gerechtigkeit.[4]

The composition of "Der Turm," "Blaue Hortensie," and "Archaischer Torso Apollos," "Der Panther," "Die letzte Graf von Brederode," and the "Selbstbildnis aus dem Jahre 1906" is presaged in this passage. And while each poem is noteworthy, the "Selbstbildnis" is unusually interesting, both in relation to the preceding remark in Rilke's letter and to a certain aspect of the art of Rodin.

During Rilke's tenure as secretary to Rodin, he learned a great deal about human anatomy. In addition, through his observation of live models and Rodin's limb-by-limb construction of statues, Rilke became sensitive to the varying potentialities and the distinct

---

the deepest self-control for the sake of working. I must learn to work, to work, Lou, I am so deficient in that."

4   "Only things speak to me. Rodin's things, the things on the Gothic cathedrals, things of antiquity, all things that are complete and perfect things . . . . I am beginning to see things in a new way: flowers are often so infinitely much to me, and from animals an extraordinary excitement comes over me. And already I'm sometimes experiencing people in this way, hands are living somewhere, mouths are speaking, and I look at everything more quietly and with greater justice."

personalities, as it were, of different parts of the body. Rodin's studio was at all times strewn with plaster legs, arms, feet, torsos, heads, and hands, especially hands, each one distinct from every other. Not all of them were discarded fragments or studies in detail, for Rodin was one of the first sculptors of the twentieth century to exhibit incomplete human figures and detached limbs as finished works. Rilke could not have helped being struck by such works as "Large Left Hand of a Burgher," "Hand of Eustache-de-St-Pierre," "Hand of God," and "Torso of the Walking Man." Rilke's awareness of the autonomous existence of hands, mouths, and torsos is reflected in his letters of the period and, still more importantly, in the "Selbstbildnis aus dem Jahre 1906."

The title of the poem suggests not poetry but a kind of portraiture, not a form of literary expression, but a genre belonging traditionally to the visual arts. The title of the poem calls to mind a mirror, an easel, a palette, and brushes. One imagines a cramped Parisian garret passing for a studio and a gaunt young man in bohemian dress. One sees how his glance moves from mirror to canvas, canvas to mirror, and back again; how his arm reaches towards the canvas; a paint-laden brush ready to strike. At the outset, Rilke upsets the reader's expectations by assigning the tasks of pictorial representation to this brief poem. Not only does this action complicate one's reading of the text—it also poses special difficulties for the poet not to be met with in the writing of more conventional poetry. There is, for instance, the problem of verisimilitude. Is this a good likeness or not? Also, one might ask if it is possible to duplicate the effects of representative art in literary form.

The structure of the poem is a sonnet composed of fourteen lines which rhymes in an unusual A-B-B-A-B-B-A-A-B-C-D-D-D-C pattern.[5] The first nine lines are devoted purely to a description of

---

5   Des alten lange adligen Geschlechtes
     Feststehendes im Augenbogenbau.
     Im Blicke noch der Kindheit Angst und Blau
     und Demut da und dort, nicht eines Knechtes

the subject, that is, the author's face. The last five lines begin with an analysis—objective observation detached in tone—of character based on the preceding description. The poem ends with a prediction of the subject's future. The image created in the first section of the poem is not, however, complete. Only a few outstanding features— the eyebrows, eyes, mouth, and forehead—are actually described. (The rest—the nose, ears, and chin—are notably absent from Rilke's self-portrait.) These are sketched in rapidly as if with a few spare lines of charcoal or India ink. One color, blue, is dominant. The flow of descriptive modifiers is unimpeded by the superintending presence of verbs. The overall effect produced is one of balance and proportion, of the fittingness of the parts to the whole, much like the impact a well-formed face ought to have on the beholder.

The most important feature of the face, as it is represented in the poem, coming first and leaving a lasting impression, are the eyebrows, whose "archingness" expresses the nobility of an old family as embodied in the last part of the line:

> Das alten lange adligen Geschlechtes
> Feststehendes im Augenbogenbau.[6]

Next come the eyes, or rather, Rilke's description of the dreamy gaze of the subject, in which his childhood anxieties and childlike innocence (preserved in the undiluted blue of his eyes), as well as humility, remain fresh and vivid:

> doch eines Dienenden und einer Frau.
> Der Mund als Mund gemacht, groß und genau,
> nicht überredend, aber ein Gerechtes
> Aussagendes. Die Stirne ohne Schlechtes
> und gern im Schatten stiller Niederschau.
>
> Das, als Zusammenhang, erst nur geahnt;
> noch nie im Leiden oder im Gelingen
> zusammengefaßt zu dauerndem Durchdringen,
> doch so, als wäre mit zerstreuten Dingen
> von fern ein Ernstes, Wirkliches geplant.

6   "The ancient noble lineage/Fixed in the eyebrows."

> Im Blicke noch der Kindheit Angst und Blau
> und Demut da und dort, nicht eines Knechtes,
> doch eines Dienenden und einer Frau.[7]

Here again, as in the characterization of the eyebrows, Rilke is less concerned with the eyes themselves than with the quality of their gaze and the portents they contain. Arriving at the mouth, which not only occupies the anatomical center of the face, but also the midpoint of the poem, Rilke fixes his attention on this significant organ itself:

> Der Mund als Mund gemacht, gross und genau,
> nicht überredend, aber ein Gerechtes Aussagendes.[8]

This is clearly a poet's mouth, not belonging to a diplomat or a businessman. It is a mouth not prudent enough to withhold the truth and, unlike the eyebrows and eyes, enjoys a kind of autonomous existence apart from the other facial features, which seem to exist to frame and support the mouth. The mouth enjoys this splendid privilege since it is potentially the oracle of truth and the instrument of the poet's voice. The autonomy of the mouth in Rilke's self-portrait suggests that the existence of the poet is derived from unmediated being rather than through conditionality or subservience, as is the case of the heavily modified eyebrows, eyes, and forehead, and sets it apart from the portraits of painters (and even Greek sculptors), in which the emphasis is nearly always on the eyes, the organs of vision.

Rilke describes his forehead last of all. It is broad, dignified, unblemished, and full of thought:

> Die Stirne ohne Schlechtes
> und gern im Schatten stiller Niederschau.[9]

---

7   "In the look still childhood fear and blue/And humility here and there, not of a farmhand/Yet of a servant and a woman."
8   "The mouth made as a mouth, large and precise,/Not persuasive, but a just statement."
9   The forehead without blemish/Gladly lies in the shadow of the still lowered glance."

The forehead is tilted at a contemplative angle. At this point, Rilke indicates a pause before revealing, in the last five lines, the outcome of his serene observations: "Das, als Zusammenhand, erst nur geahnt." Having finished his examination of the individual features of his face, Rilke suddenly notices how they fit together to form a whole:

> noch nie im Leiden oder im Gelingen
> zusammengefaßt zu dauerdem Durchdringen,
> doch so, als wäre mit zerstreuten Dingen
> von fern ein Ernstes, Wirkliches geplant.[10]

Rilke realizes that, up to the present moment, all his sorrows and successes have been fleeting and insufficient. He sees how they have been mere preparation for a real and serious future endeavor, which now looms in the distance, foreign and uncertain. And yet, he is secure in the knowledge that his working methods have attained new discipline and greater clarity by his association with Rodin.

---

10   Never in suffering or in success/Summarized to permanent penetration,/But as if with scattered things,/Something serious and real, planned from afar.

5   Three Modernist Poets and the Search for Cultural Rebirth

> "After one has abandoned a belief in God, poetry is that essence which takes its place in life's redemption . . . . In an age of disbelief, or, what is the same thing, in a time that is largely humanistic, in one sense or another, it is for the poet to supply the satisfactions of belief."
>
> Wallace Stevens, *"Two or Three Ideas"*

The abundance of manifestoes and credos that accompanied the publication of Modernist poetry is symptomatic of the insecurity of modern poets who felt it necessary to explain their methods and goals to an audience bewildered by an array of recondite mythologies and disruptive techniques. In their poetry and criticism, Osip Mandelstam (1891–1938), Rainer Maria Rilke (1875–1926), and David Jones (1895–1974) seek to define the relationship of the poet to history and the present time as the medium in which to foster a cultural rebirth and confirmation of the cultural leadership of the poet. The present essay is an effort to make explicit connections between these three poets and their cultural programs.

The unifying force in poetry which links the culture of the past with the present is, of course, language. It is the task of the modern poet to perceive the unity and continuity of life and to preserve that unity and continuity for posterity by conferring literary form upon the flux of life. Mandelstam, however, believed that "the pass to poetry is granted only by faith in its sacramental character and a sense of responsibility for everything that happens in the world."[1] Mandelstam called on all artists and writers to join in the crusade against nihilism, in the redemption of the earth, in "sowing grain

---

1   Quoted by Nadezhda Mandelstam, *Hope Abandoned* (New York: Athenaum, 1974), 96.

through the ether" to satiate the "hunger in interplanetary space."[2] Among artists, "there is no equality, there is no competition, there is only the complicity of all who conspire against emptiness and non-existence."[3]

Mandelstam was joined by other poets who had more in common than a shared concern for the renewal of culture and an appreciation of disciplined, muscular poetry. Their humanist credo was given the title of "Acmeism," and it signaled a renewed appreciation for things—not as symbols pointing to a higher order of reality but as objects in their own right—whose innate qualities rather than mystical attributes make them interesting to the poet. In the words of literary historian Marc Slonim, the Acmeists "rejected the priority of musicality in symbolist poetry, the obscurity of its vocabulary, the dimness of its allusions and shadowy flights toward unknown worlds and unseen signs of the absolute."[4] Fellow Acmeist, Sergej Gorodetsky (1884–1967), put the matter this way: "We wish to admire a rose because it is beautiful, not because it is the symbol of mystical purity."[5] No longer would the poet make obeisance to the "unknown," nor attempt to capture what cannot be comprehended. Beauty and meaning were henceforward to be sought for in concrete realities. For Gorodetsky and Mandelstam (as well as their colleagues Anna Akhmatova and Nikolaj Gumiljov), the relationship of the poet to his subject is analogous to that of an artisan and his precious materials or an architect and his blueprints. The artist "considers his world view a tool and an instrument, like a

2   "Word and Culture," *Mandelstam: The Complete Critical Prose and Letters,* ed. Jane Gary Harris (Ann Arbor: Ardis, 1979), 116. Hereafter cited as *Mandelstam.*

3   "Morning of Acmeism," *Mandelstam,* 64.

4   Marc Slonim, *Soviet Russian Literature* (New York: Oxford UP, 1977, 2nd ed., rev.), 250. See also Stephen Broyde, *Osip Mandelstam and His Age* (Cambridge: Harvard UPO, 1975), Clare Cavanagh, *Osip Mandelstam and the Modern Creation of Tradition* (Princeton: Princeton UP, 1995), and Jane Gary Harris, *Osip Mandelstam* (Boston: G.K. Hall, 1988).

5   Quoted by Nikolaj Gumiljov in "Symbolism's Legacy and Acmeism," *The Silver Age of Russian Culture,* ed. Carl and Ellendea Proffer (Ann Arbor: Ardis, 1975). Hereafter cited as *Gumiljov.*

hammer in the hands of a stonemason, and his only reality is the work of art itself . . . . Acmeism is for those who, seized with the spirit of building, do not renounce their own gravity, but joyously accept it in order to awaken and use the forces architecturally sleeping in it. The architect says: I build, that is to say, I am right."[6]

The poet must obey the laws of nature and recognize that the "first condition of successful building" is "genuine piety before the three dimensions of space."[7] In addition, the poet must achieve an "abundance of life, a sense of organic wholeness, and an active equilibrium" — in short, a greater balance of "forces" than that observed in Symbolist poetry.[8] While admiring the virtuosity of the Symbolists for creating sublime euphonic effects and for having shown "the significance of the symbol of art," Mandelstam did not concur in "offering up in sacrifice to it all other manners of poetic effect," but sought "their complete coordination."[9]

Just as integral to Acmeism as the notion of organic wholeness is the need to restore the primary status of "the word as such."[10] For too long the "conscious sense" of the word, the Logos, had been subordinated to the other elements of the word, of which the most important, as far as Symbolism was concerned, had been its phonic husk. But for Mandelstam, "the conscious sense" of the word, the Logos, is just as splendid a form as music is for the Symbolists."[11] By rescuing the kernel of the word from the Symbolist threshing floor, Mandelstam claims that Acmeism has at the same time bestowed a hitherto unparalleled measure of nobility on the word: "And if, among the Futurists, the word as such is still creeping on all fours, in Acmeism it has for the first time assumed a more dignified vertical position and entered upon the stone age of its

---

6   "Morning of Acmeism," *Mandelstam*, 45–46.
7   *Ibid.*
8   "On the Nature of the Word," *Mandelstam*, 121.
9   *Gumiljov*, 51.
10   "Morning of Acmeism," *Mandelstam*, 45.
11   *Ibid.*

existence."[12] With Acmeism humankind returned from exile and re-gained their earthly paradise. Humanity stood at the center of the Acmeist universe, and Mandelstam is concerned above all with hu-man endeavors and the products of human handicraft: the culti-vated earth, its orchards and fields, manmade objects and edifices. "Hellenism" is Mandelstam's collective name for the processes of domestication and acculturation that proceeded from humankind's efforts in the distant past to conquer the external world:

> Hellenism is an earthenware pot, oven tongs, a milk jug, kitchen utensils, dishes; it is anything which surrounds the body; Hellenism is the warmth of the hearth experienced as something sacred; it is anything which imparts some of the external world to man . . . . Hellenism is the conscious surrounding of man with domestic utensils instead of impersonal objects; the transformation of impersonal objects into domestic utensils, and the humanization and warming of the surrounding world with the most delicate teleological warmth. Hellenism is any kind of stove near which a man sits, treasuring its heat as something akin to his own internal body heat.[13]

Mandelstam identified the "moving force of Acmeism" with "the indomitable will to create" a human-centered poetics, with humans as masters of their world, "not flattened into a wafer by the horrors of pseudo-Symbolism."[14] Rejecting the otherworldliness of Symbol-ist "correspondences," the poetry of Acmeism strove to become "a genuine Symbolism surrounded by genuine symbols, that is, by do-mestic utensils having their own verbal representations, just as hu-mans have their own vital organs."[15]

Mandelstam claimed that Acmeism was not just a "literary phenomenon in Russian history," but "a social force" as well. "With Acmeism," he insists, "a moral force was reborn in Russian po-etry."[16] That moral force was humanism, and Acmeism offered as a counterforce to the "anarchistic, nihilistic" spirit of the nineteenth

---

12 *Ibid.*
13 "On the Nature of the Word," *Mandelstam,* 127–128.
14 *Ibid.,* 131.
15 *Ibid.*
16 *Ibid.*

century, with its legacy of dehumanization in literature and its poetry of homelessness and alienation, the artistic and ethical heritage
of Greco-Roman antiquity and Renaissance Italy. The difference between the "Hellenization" of antiquity and Mandelstam's "inner
Hellenism" lay in the singular requirements needed to remedy
modern humanity's perceived spiritual desolation and alienation
from the natural world. What is required to mend the fragmentation of the age? Who is able to restore integrity to the search for
external equivalents to one's inmost feelings and aspirations?

To tear this time into freedom, to begin a new world, Mandelstam insists, in the poem "My Age" (1922), that what is needed is "a
flute to tie up/the joints of the knotty days"—the poet's song, the
golden, redemptive song of life will exhort the buds to swell with
moisture and green shoots to splash out of the rejuvenated earth. The
power of regeneration belongs to the poets. They will restore life to
the culture of an epoch alienated from the past. The effort will not be
easy, the stakes are terribly high, but the poet cannot afford not to try:

> . . . Take courage, men!
> While we're cutting the ocean, like a plow; even
> In Lethe's cold hard frost, we'll remember
> That earth was worth ten heavens to us.[17]

In these lines is heard the voice of the mature Aristotelian who finds
it unthinkable that this world should be forsaken, however imperfect it may appear beside the realm of eternal ideas. We also hear
an echo of the lines of the young Mandelstam who wrote, "I love
my poor earth/because I have seen no other."[18] It is the voice as well
as of Mandelstam, the disciple of Nietzsche, who, like Achilles,
would prefer eternal servitude on earth to absolute authority in an
incorporeal realm, and who is confident that even on the journey
across the cold, forbidding stream of the river Lethe, his memory
will not be purged of his earthly experience.

---

17   Mandelstam, "The Twilight of Freedom" (1913).
18   Mandelstam, "To read only children's books" (1908).

Mandelstam believed that the fate of the earth was bound up with the fate of humanity and its poetic culture, at the center of which stands the beleaguered citadel of language. Western civilization is surrounded by a wilderness inhabited by hostile tribes of barbarians who threaten to storm the gates:

> We have no Acropolis. Even today our culture is wandering and finding its walls. Nevertheless, each word in Dal's [Russian] dictionary is a kernel of the Acropolis, a small kremlin, a winged fortress of nominalism, rigged out in the Hellenic spirit for the relentless battle against the formless element, against non-existence, which threatens history from every side.[19]

In an attempt to raise the siege, Zarathustra marshalled his army of yea-sayers, Rilke's "bees of inwardness" provided sweet sustenance, and Mandelstam led the vanguard of Acmeism. For the dual tasks of redeeming the earth and restoring vitality to culture, humankind had to become studier and more resilient than anything else in the world. Unlike Russian civic poetry of the nineteenth century, or its contemporary Soviet equivalent, the aesthetic ethos of Acmeism had no room for a poetry that set out merely to make good citizens of its readers. "There is a loftier principle than *Citizen*," Mandelstam insisted. "There is the concept of *Man*."[20] The Spartan regimen prescribed by Acmeism reflects the demands of an age of revolution, world and civil war, along with moral, aesthetic, and philosophical upheaval: "The ideal of perfect manliness is provided by the style and practical demands of the age. Everything has become heavier and more massive; thus, man must become harder, for he must be the hardest thing on earth; he must be to the earth what the diamond is to glass."[21] Or what poetry is to the soil of time. In spite of the increasing fragmentation of traditional sources of meaning, accompanied by the destabilization caused by economic insecurity and the rise political dictatorship, Mandelstam does not relinquish an anthropomorphic

---

19 "On the Nature of the Word," *Mandelstam*, 126.
20 *Ibid.*, 132.
21 *Ibid.*

bias in his work. Humankind is not only the measure of meaning in world history, but its teleology and fullest expression. As Nadezhda Mandelstam confirmed in later years, the central idea "running through the whole of Mandelstam's poetry is that of man as the hub and embodiment of existence . . . and of mankind as the summation of life's meaning."[22] The task for humanity is to build, to conquer and fill emptiness, to keep alive the memory of its greatest achievements, to leave tangible traces of its presence in art and labors: to defeat time and death, if only in the shape of time-worn brass horseshoes or clipped gold coins. While Franz Kafka wrote modern allegories of the fall, Mandelstam urged humankind to take up residence again in the garden; while Ludwig Wittgenstein probed the limits of language, Mandelstam praised the unbounded potential of the word; while Thomas Mann ironically depicted the disintegration of European bourgeois culture, Mandelstam sought to remedy the moral and aesthetic decadence of the age.

Mandelstam's view of the poet's large duties is comparable to the poetic vocations of Rainer Maria Rilke and David Jones, poets who also believed in the sacred and redemptive properties of poetry. In the *Duineser Elegien* [*Duino Elegies*] (1923) Rilke sets out, in the wake of the perceived collapse of the traditional hierarchy of values, to reinterpret the world anew, and redeem the earth for humankind through his voice. The point of embarkation for this cycle of poems consists in that abyss of nothingness that is felt where once was an articulated vision of man's place in the world:

> . . . Ach, wen vermögen
> wir denn zu brauchen? Engel nicht, Menschen nicht,
> und die findigen Tiere merken es schon,
> daß wir nicht sehr verläßlich zu Haus sind,
> in der gedeuteten Welt.[23]

---

22 *Hope Abandoned*, 536.
23 "Die Erste Elegie": Ah, who could we/Possibly need then? Not angels, not people,/And the resourceful animals have already noticed,/That we are not very reliably at home,/In the interpreted world.

"Whom can we make use of?" in the task of assuring ourselves of being at home in an interpreted world? The task requires courage and involves not only a Nietzschean "transvaluation of values" in the search for a valid and meaningful new order, but a transformation of the external world, in which even the beasts are aware of our human uneasiness. "Wen vermögen wir denn zu brauchen?" That is, what is the human faculty by which we are integrated into life? Descartes and Leibniz answer this question in similar ways ("Cogito ergo sum"), not in a physical sense, but in the metaphysical sense that Rilke invokes angels as the embodiment of the highest order of being. The terror of an angel's approach poses a challenge for humankind to reshape itself through a process of mind that would gradually encompass and then transform the earth. Until the renewal of the earth is complete, human experience will continue along an axis of disorientation with the result that one's sense of belonging in the world will be transient, and one's sense of spiritual well-being will be elusive and conveyed by random receptacles of meaning that one happens to chance upon:

> . . . Es bleibt uns vielleicht
> irgend ein Baum an dem Abhang, daß wir ihn täglich
> wiedersähen; es bleibt uns die Straße von gestern
> und das verzogene Treusein einer Gewohnheit,
> der es bei uns gefiel, und so blieb sie und ging nicht.[24]

While the task of humankind in antiquity had been to domesticate the external world, the challenge facing modern poets is not concerned with "Hellenization" *per se* but rather involves what might be called the conquest of an "inner Hellenism." The discovery and colonization of inwardness, the need, in Mandelstam's phrase, "to conquer emptiness, to hypnotize space," the comfortable furnishing

---

24   "Die erste Elegie": Perhaps there will be/Some tree left on the slope,/That we will see every day;/We are left with the road from yesterday/And the spoiled loyalty to a habit,/That we enjoyed, and so it stayed and didn't go.

of our inner dimension; all are aspects of the task of injecting new meaning and significance into a world depleted of spiritual content.[25]

However, this furnishing of humanity's inner circle with monuments of spiritual fullness, this infusion of the earth with the "teleological warmth" of the hearth is not easily accomplished when the outer world is no longer as accessibly meaningful to the poet as in other times:

> Nirgends, Geliebte, wird Welt sein, als innen. Unser
> Leben geht hin mit Verwandlung. Und immer geringer
> schwindet das Außen. Wo einmal ein dauerndes Haus war,
> schlägt sich erdachtes Gebild vor, quer, zu Erdenklichem
> völlig gehörig, als stand es noch ganz im Gehirne.[26]

From now on, the poet must seek to extol the growing edifice of his own inner spiritual development:

> . . . Ja, wo noch eins übersteht,
> ein einst gebetetes Ding, eingedientes, geknietes,
> hält es sich, so wie es ist, schon ins Unsichtbare hin.
> Viele gewahres nicht mehr, doch ohne den Vorteil,
> daß sie's nun *innerlich* baun, mit Pfeilen und Statuen, größer![27]

As Erich Heller explains, things approach the poet, "asking to be taught how to become words and how to make themselves truly felt in the widened space, and in return they show him that this is precisely his real task in the world; to assimilate them into the new

---

25 "Morning of Acmeism," *Mandelstam*, 63.
26 "Die siebente Elegie": Nowhere, beloved, will the world be but within. Our/Life disappears with transformation. And always smaller/The outside world disappears. Where once there was a permanent house,/An imaginary image is suggested, across to the imaginable/Completely belongs, as if it were still present in the brain.
27 "Die siebente Elegie": Yes, where we still survive,/A thing that once prayed, served, kneeled,/If it stays where it is, already in the invisible,/Many are no longer aware, but the advantage,/That they now build it within, with arrows and statues, but so much greater!

inward dimension."[28] In the "Ninth Elegy," Rilke announces the
new responsibility of the poet in the form of an urgent question:

> ... Sind wir vielleicht *hier*, um zu sagen: Haus,
> Brücke, Brunnen, Tor, Krug, Obstbaum, Fenster,—
> höchstens: Säule, Turm ... aber zu *sagen*, verstehs,
> oh zu sagen so, wie selber die Dinge niemals
> innig meinten zu sein.[29]

A house poised on a hill surrounded by a grove of olive or fruit
trees, a fountain splashing in a village square, an earthenware jug
brimful of viscous honey, an open window pouring music out onto
a statue garden, a delicate seashell lying on a foamy stretch of sand,
a spool of lace—these objects are fragmentary symbols of Mandelstam's and Rilke's tenuously humanized world. Pillars and towers
are architectural vestiges of the most humane but lost civilizations,
the Greco-Roman world and the Renaissance. For Mandelstam the
distinguishing sign of these periods in history was their expression
of "genuine piety before the three dimensions of space." In Peri-
clean Athens, Augustan Rome, and the Florence of the Medicis, the
earth was regarded "neither as a burden nor as unfortunate acci-
dent, but as a God-given palace."[30]

Rilke realized that the poetic enterprise of the *Neue Gedichte*—
the effort to express the poetical essence of things as if things themselves opened their mouths to say what they were—had been su-
perseded. The problem now facing the poet, as Heller explains, is
the transformation of "the doomed external world-doomed not
merely through present technologies and future wars; but through

---

28   Erich Heller, "Rilke and Nietzsche," *The Disinherited Mind* (New York: Harcourt, Brace, Jovanovich, 1975), 143.

29   "Die neunte Elegie": Perhaps we are here to say: house,/Bridge, fountain, gate,
jug, fruit tree, window,—/At most: columns, tower ... but to *say*, understand,/Oh, to say of things in a way that they themselves never intended in-
wardly to be.

30   "Morning of Acmeism," *Mandelstam*, 63.

the diminution of its spiritual value-into pure inwardness."[31] As Rilke writes in a letter of 1917, "I must assume that our experiences are shifting further into the invisible, into the bacillary and microscopic . . . . The earth has no other refuge except to become invisible in us . . . only in us can this intimate and enduring transformation of the Visible into the Invisible . . . be accomplished."[32] The urgent command the poet received was the transformation of the physical world, its purification in the fire of subjectivity, and its resurrection in inwardness:

> Erde, ist es nicht dies, was du willst: *unsichtbar*
> in uns erstehn?—Ist es dein Traum nicht,
> einmal unsichtbar zu sein?—Erde! unsichtbar!
> Was, wenn Verwandlung nicht, ist dein drängener Auftrag?[33]

Rilke's "inner spaces"—*Weltinnenraum*—is a world from which time is excluded, in which all real things and monuments of culture subsist side by side in a kind of magic contemporaneity. This world corresponds to a remarkable degree to Mandelstam's understanding of Henri Bergson's concept of *durée* [duration] and how it can be applied to art and history in that time requires images and objects to escape the ineffable:

> Bergson does not consider phenomena according to the way they submit to the law of temporal succession, but rather according to their spatial extension. He is interested exclusively in the internal connection among phenomena. He liberates this connection from time and considers it independently. Phenomena thus connected to one another form, as it were, a kind of fan whose folds can be opened up in time.[34]

---

31   Erich Heller, "The Poet in the Age of Prose: Reflections on Hegel's Aesthetics and Rilke's Duino Elegies," *In the Age of Prose* (Cambridge: Cambridge UP, 1984), 9.

32   *Wartime Letters of Rainer Maria Rilke*, trans. M.D. Herter Norton (New York: W.W. Norton and Co., 1968), 74.

33   "Die neunte Elegie:" Earth, isn't this what you desire: invisibly/To rise in us? Isn't that your dream?/To be invisible once? Earth? Invisible?/What, if not this metamorphosis, is this not your most urgent missio

34   "On the Nature of the Word," *Mandelstam*, 117.

Unimpeded by the drag of time, this enduring presentation of cultural phenomena across the millenia unfolds in "interplanetary space," in *Weltinnenraum,* and unites the contemporary poet with kindred spirits from every historical epoch. In this way, Mandelstam can make the seemingly outlandish demand, "I want Ovid, Pushkin, and Catullus to live once more and am not satisfied with the historical Ovid, Pushkin, and Catullus."[35] To bring them to life again, the poet must understand how "the passing moment can . . . endure the pressure of centuries and preserve itself intact, remaining forever the same 'here and now.' You need only know how to extract that 'here and now' from the soil of Time without harming its roots, or it will wither and die."[36] As assiduously as Mandelstam, Rilke plows the fertile fields of history and disinters the extinct race of heroes, resurrects the great lovers Orpheus and Eurydice, and those self-masters, the youthfully dead. In Mandelstam and Rilke's imaginations it is as if the pantheon of Mount Parnassus comes alive in a perpetual classical *Walpurgisnacht.*

The essence of Mandelstam's "Hellenism" and Rilke's *Weltinnenraum* is contained in David Jones's notion of art as sacrament: an anthropomorphic interpretation of experience, a belief in the salvation of the world that can be achieved through the humanizing power of civilization, and confidence that the artist's creations point to humanity's participation in eternity, "in a without endness." Among the three poets discussed in this essay, Jones is the sole Christian believer; Mandelstam is a classical humanist and Rilke is a non-sectarian aesthete whose angel is an intermediary between the poet and his muse. Unlike many Modernist poets, Jones does not feel the urgency to invent a new religious mythology as a means of interpreting the alienating, disorienting experience of modern life. Instead, Jones relies on Christianity to illuminate the place of humans in the world and to meet their spiritual aspirations.

---

35   "François Villon," *Mandelstam,* 58.
36   *Ibid.*

And yet, Jones's faith does not remove his pessimism about the present phase in Western civilization. From his perspective, which is Spenglerian in its emphasis on progressive decline, religion and art are the chief victims of culture's disintegration:

> Today we live in a world where the symbolic life (the life of the true cultures, of "institutional" religion, and of *all artists*) is progressively eliminated — the technician is master . . . . The priest and the artist are already in the catacombs, but *separate* catacombs — for the technician divides to rule.[37]

In Jones's view, religion and art are products of a unified psychological response to humans' metaphysical astonishment at their own mortality and the bewildering suspicion that some part of each individual nevertheless endures for all eternity. Religion is the ideal aspect and art is the concrete manifestation of this metaphysical understanding of existence. Whenever a person seeks to give expression to religious feelings the inevitable result is an artifact that points to the absolute and reflects the enduring aspect of human existence. In this way, art and religion are linked ideally and *in praxis*. To sever the bonds between them would be untold damage to the delicate equilibrium of the human psyche and to disrupt the balance of contending forces in civilization. Jones is convinced that without "a corporate tradition there can be no corporate renewal," which suggests that in the absence of the religious ligatures holding art within an interpreted view of reality, which grants the artist freedom of movement within an interpreted world, the result is "corpse rather than *corpus*."[38]

Jones is aware that at present "we are . . . very far removed from those culture-phases where the poet was explicitly and by profession the custodian, rememberer, embodier, and voice of the mythus" — that is, the ethos, the "whole *res* [reality] of which the poet is himself a product."[39] His effort to reclaim the poet's cultural

---

37   David Jones, "Religion and the Muses," *Epoch and Artist* (London: Faber and Faber, 1959), 103. Hereafter cited as *Epoch*.
38   Jones, "Art and Sacrament" and "Religion and the Muses," *Epoch*, 159, 105.
39   Jones, "The Preface to *The Anathemata*," *Epoch*, 117.

authority is reminiscent of similar statements by William Wordsworth in the "Preface" to *Lyrical Ballads* (1798) and by Percy Bysshe
Shelley in *A Defence of Poetry* (1822) one hundred years previously.
In the long poem, *The Anathemata,* Jones, unlike Mandelstam or
Rilke, who look to the future for the hopeful signs of cultural renewal, looks back to earlier periods in history — "culture-phases" —
the Stone Age, Greek Antiquity, the early Middle Ages, and to an
imagined prelapsarian blossom time of human culture, all of which,
he claims to have been characterized by Schillerian *Naivität* or authenticity — "where the poet as sign-maker and artificer, as a privi-
leged interpreter of experience and the society in which he lived
shared an enclosed and common background, where the terms of
reference were common to all."[40]

The landscape of *The Anathemata,* which is inhabited by figures
from British and Celtic mythology, Greek gods, heroes, and great
beauties, is nonetheless not very distant from Mandelstam's Berg-
sonian idea of "interplanetary space" or Rilke's *Weltinnenraum* or
"inner space." All three locations are sanctuaries for the beleaguered refugees of the modern wars between the busy external
world and human inwardness. In these regions of the mind the artist is still able to unite the normally opposed spheres of the sacred
and the profane, cosmos and chaos, symbol and reality. Here the
sanctity of manufactured (handmade) objects, revered souvenirs of
natural origin, and primordial rituals — all "tokens, the matrices, the
institutes, the ancilia, the fertile ashes, the phallic foreshadowings:
the things come down from heaven together with the kept memo-
rials, the things lifted up and the venerated trinkets" — has been
preserved.[41] In his search for signs of the emergence of *homo sapiens,*
the species that is by definition a maker of signs, Jones speculates
on the artistic and religious significance of Neanderthal burial practices that surely followed other even more ancient paradigms:

---

40   *Ibid.,* 111.
41   Jones, *The Anathemata* (London: Faber and Faber, 1979), 50.

What, from this one's cranial data,
is like to have been his kindred's
psyche; in that they along
with the journey-food, donated
the votive horn? and with what
pietas did they donate these
among the dead, the life-givers
and by what rubric?
And before them? those who put on their coats to oblate
the things set apart in an older Great Cold.[42]

Converging in the primordial rites of worship is the *Erhebung* of an ordinary object to the status of a work of art:

By the uteral marks
that makes the covering stone an artefact.
By the penile ivory
And by the viatic meats.
Dona ei requiem[43]

What momentous event, analogous to the catastrophic arrival of an Ice Age, caused a rupture between the work of the poet and the needs of society, the art and the temper of the age? This is the "abiding dilemma" informing *The Anathemata* with contemporary philosophical and social relevance. For Jones, the renewal of modern culture, the reintegration of humankind, nature, and the supernatural, is to be brought about by erecting a sign—his poem—that would be valid in our universe, our world, for us in our lives, still, now. It is clear, however, that sweeping changes "in the character and orientation and nature of our civilization," must be made before we can expect the reappearance of more than a few isolated examples, such as *The Anathemata,* of an "integrated, widespread, religious art."[44]

Until such time that cultural renewal is accomplished the mission of the poet will continue to be difficult because the repositories of traditional values and themes of poetry have been broken open,

---

42   *Ibid.,* 61–62
43   *Ibid.,* 65.
44   "Religion and the Muses," *Epoch,* 103.

ransacked, and scattered by the unfriendly barbarian agents of time. The poet will search in vain for shared symbols and beliefs with which to ground his signs. Without a common mythology the poet cannot write with confidence that he is being understood by his readers; such confidence had been taken for granted in poetry's halcyon days. In the end, "the artist finds himself, willy-nilly, unintegrated with the present civilization-phase."[45] Since humans are their most human when they are making or consuming art, one can expect to find the most human "civilization-phases" where man-the-artist has not been alienated from society, where the artist's creations serve as the most fitting expressions of the character of the age. Hope for the future lies in the reintegration of the poet-artist and civilization, in curtailing antagonism between art and life, and in the renewed possibility of a return to humankind's true vocation as artist.

---

45   "Past and Present," *Epoch*, 139.

Part II

Essays in Cultural Politics

6 William Godwin:
A Life in Literature and Politics

> "[P]oetical readers have commonly remarked Milton's evil
> to be a being of considerable virtue . . . . But why did he re-
> bel against his maker? It was, as he himself informs us, be-
> cause he saw no sufficient reason, for that extreme inequal-
> ity of rank and power, which the creator assumed . . . . After
> his fall, why did he still cherish the spirit of opposition?
> From a persuasion that he was hardly and injuriously
> treated. He was not discouraged by the apparent inequality
> of the contest: because a sense of reason and justice was
> stronger in his mind, than a sense of brute force; because he
> had much of the feelings of an Epictetus or a Cato, and little
> of those of a slave."
>
> *Political Justice I: 323–325*

A protean intellectual, William Godwin enjoyed a career that reflects in microcosm the changing face of literature, society, and politics in Great Britain from the onset of the French Revolution to the
end of the Romantic age (1789–1832). The prophet of a future political order founded on justice and reason was the author of haunting
psychological novels and a vast amount of intellectual prose. Godwin's writings—along with those of Johann Wolfgang von Goethe,
his nearly exact contemporary, and Percy Bysshe Shelley, his son-
in-law—effectively combine creative imagination and philosophical speculation. He is best remembered for his controversial philosophical treatise, *An Enquiry Concerning Political Justice* (1793), and
for *Things as they are; or, The Adventures of Caleb Williams* (1794), a
precursor of the novels of Fyodor Dostoyevski and Franz Kafka as
well as modern detective fiction. In addition, he wrote five other
very long novels, a monumental biography of Geoffrey Chaucer, a
history of Commonwealth England, several plays, school texts,
children's books, political pamphlets, and a vast correspondence.

Following the publication of *Political Justice,* Godwin was much
in demand in radical political and literary circles. It was at such

gatherings that he met prominent contemporaries, including Thomas Paine (1737–1809), Samuel Taylor Colerige (1772–1834), Charles Lamb (1775–1834), William Hazlitt (1778–1830), Henry Crabb Robinson (1775–1867), and Godwin's future wife, the feminist philosopher and writer Mary Wollstonecraft (1759–1797). Noted as a nurturing presence in the lives of his friends, Godwin was a mentor to many in the first generation of Romantic writers and a leading spokesman for their political investments and moral sympathies.

Associated most closely with him are his daughter, Mary Wollstonecraft Godwin (1797–1851), and her husband, the poet Percy Bysshe Shelley (1792–1822). Godwin's central teaching that the world could be transformed by dint of rational argument, overwhelming empirical evidence, and charismatic personal leadership persuaded the young scholar Shelley to distribute his pamphlet *The Necessity of Atheism* (1811), which led to his expulsion from Oxford University. Shelley, in Leslie Stephen's retelling, "greeted the writings of Godwin as the lost traveler greets a beacon-fire on a stormy night. They seemed to contain a new gospel."[1] Shelley's initial letters to Godwin convey his relief at finding him still among the living and embody the devotee's enthusiastic embrace of his idol:

> I had enrolled your name in the lists of the honourable dead. I had felt regret that the glory of your being had passed from this earth of ours. It is not so; you still live and, I firmly believe, are still planning the welfare of human kind . . . . Guide thou and direct me. In all the weakness of my inconsistencies bear with me . . . when you reprove me, reason speaks; I acquiesce in her decisions (January 3, 1811).

Shelley confesses that *Political Justice* "opened to my mind fresh and more extensive views; it materially influenced my character, and I rose from its perusal a wiser and a better man."[2] There is, moreover, an unacknowledged but natural connection between Godwin's

---

1   Leslie Stephen, "Godwin and Shelley," *Hours in a Library*, 3 Volumes (London: Smith, Elder & Company, 1899), Vol. III, 64.

2   *Letters from P.B. Shelley to William Godwin* (London: Privately Printed, 1891), 4–5.

views on marriage and social equality—as set forth in *Political Justice*—and Pantisocracy, Coleridge and Robert Southey's failed scheme to build an ideal community on the banks of the Susquehanna River in Pennsylvania. In later years, Coleridge and Godwin became friends and the younger poet often sought out the greying philosopher as a sounding board for his ideas.

William Godwin was born on March 3, 1756 at Wisbech, Cambridgeshire, where his father, John, was a dissenting minister. The kindliness of William's mother, Ann Hull Godwin, offset her husband's stern demeanor. Intellectually precocious, Godwin was the seventh of thirteen children, and he was brought up according to strict puritanical principles. In 1758 John Godwin moved the family to Debenham, Suffolk, but he was forced to leave in 1760 when a vocal minority in his congregation opposed his teaching. The family finally settled in Guestwick, Norfolk, where William was sent, in 1764, to a school run by Robert Akers in nearby Hindolveston. It was there that he first began to give some indication of his intellectual capacity as well as his inclination to follow in his father's footsteps. In 1767 he became a pupil in a school run by Samuel Newton. Godwin was deeply influenced by his teacher's radical politics and strict Sandemanianism, a branch of Calvinism that emphasized the dominance of reason over emotion. In later years Godwin criticized Newton's unsparing use of the rod.

John Godwin, who did not have a close relationship with William, died on November 12, 1772, and in April 1773 William moved with his mother to London. Since dissenters could not matriculate at the universities of Oxford and Cambridge, William applied for admission to Homerton Academy, but was rejected on suspicion of holding strict Sandemanian principles. As a result, William entered the Coward Trust's Academy at Hoxton in 1773 and was tutored by the scholar and prolific writer Andrew Kippis (1725–1795), who directed his study of the classics, history, grammar, philosophy, and recent scientific discoveries. Kippis, in contrast to Newton, was a kind man who became a trusted and useful friend. While at Hoxton

Godwin was known to rise early and work at his studies far into the night, and from this regimen he acquired the philosophical views concerning materialism and necessity that, combined with his Calvinist temperament, characterize his mature writings.

Originally determined to make a career as a minister, Godwin gave a series of sermons at Yarmouth and Lowestoft in the summer of 1777. After failing in his attempt to be appointed minister at Christchurch, Hampshire, he was accepted at Ware in Hertford-shire. Here he came under the influence of Joseph Fawcett (1758–1804), a follower of Jonathan Edwards (1703–1758), the prominent philosophical theologian in colonial New England. Fawcett later made a career as a poet and a preacher. Extremely progressive in his political views, he engaged Godwin in wide-ranging discussions. In August 1779 Godwin moved to London, and then in 1780 he successfully applied to become minister at Stowmarket, Suffolk.

While he was at Stowmarket, Godwin's intellectual development took a new turn with his discovery of the writings of the satirist Jonathan Swift (1667–1745) and the French philosophers Claude-Adrien Helvétius (1715–1771), Baron Paul Henri Dietrich d'Holbach (1723–1789), and Jean-Jacques Rousseau (1712–1778). In *Political Justice*, Godwin praises Swift as possessing "more profound insight into the true principles of political justice, than any preceding or contemporary author."[3] The combination of Swiftian satire on the follies of humankind and the skepticism of the deist French philosophers dealt a fatal blow to the young minister's faith in Christianity while at the same time suggesting the notion—which was to become a leitmotiv of his later social and political teaching—that "human depravity originates in the vices of the political constitution."[4] Godwin's faith was for a time partially

---

3   William Godwin, *Enquiry Concerning Political Justice and Its Influence on Morals and Happiness* (London: G.G. and J. Robinson, 1793, rev. ed., 1798), 552.

4   William Godwin, MS List of Political Principles, cited in Mark Philp, "Introduction," *Political and Philosophical Writings of William Godwin*, gen. ed. Mark Philp, 7 vols. (London: Pickering and Chatto, 1993), Vol. I, 17.

restored by his reading of Joseph Priestly's *Institutes of Natural and Revealed Religion* (1772–1774), but in 1782 he alienated his congregation by the overtly philosophical content of his sermons. He therefore gave up the ministry and moved to London. Although he would be attached on a trial basis to the congregation at Beaconsfield during the early part of 1783, by autumn he had determined to make a living and a name for himself as a writer. Fawcett, his original mentor, endorsed this decision.

Godwin's first major published work, *The History of the Life of William Pitt, Earl of Chatham*, appeared in 1783, and while it sold few copies, it was well received by the critics of the time. Godwin then began to write pamphlets and articles and became a regular contributor to the *English Review*. His articles also appeared in the liberal *Political Herald and Review*, and he published a political pamphlet, *A Defence of the Rockingham Party, in their Late Coalition with the Right Honorable Frederic Lord North* (1783).

While Godwin's choice of a new profession engaged his time and energy, it did not provide financial security. Therefore, in June 1783, he published a prospectus for a school to be run according to the pedagogical implications of his recently adopted Rousseauian view that the essential goodness of man is corrupted by social institutions. *An Account of the Seminary that will be opened on Monday the Fourth Day of August, at Epsom in Surrey, for the Instruction of Twelve Pupils in the Greek, Latin, French, and English Languages* failed to attract a sufficient number of applicants, so Godwin's school never opened.

His next scheme—that of becoming a novelist—bore fruit with the publication of *Damon and Delia* in 1784, which deals with tragic love in a pastoral setting. In a thinly veiled allusion to Godwin's recent, involuntary departure from Stowmarket, the protagonist is a young pastor who is misunderstood and rejected by his flock. *Damon and Delia* was appreciatively received by the *English Review*, but no great success resulted. In the same year Godwin produced a selection of sermons, a volume entitled *Sketches in History*, and a bizarre pamphlet, *The Herald of Literature; or, A Review of the Most Considerable Productions that will be made in the Course of the Ensuing Winter: With Extracts,* which includes imitations, in several genres, of such popular contemporary writers as Frances Burney (1752–1840) and James Beattie (1735–1803). Any assessment of Godwin's writing to this point in his career would reveal that his interest in political and social issues is matched by his involvement with imaginative compositions.

Godwin published two more novels in 1784. The first, *Italian Letters; or, The History of The Count de St. Julian,* written in epistolary form, exposes distorted values instilled by social and economic class distinctions. *Imogen: A Pastoral Romance* was inspired by Godwin's reading of Rousseau and the popular interest in British folklore that was awakened by the phenomenal success of James Macpherson's fraudulent but wildly popular Ossian poems (first published in 1761). *Imogen* may also be seen as a precursor to Walter Scott's historical novels, in which the hardscrabble but virtuous existence led by the peasantry is contrasted with the decadent life at court.

In 1785 Andrew Kippis helped Godwin secure a position as the historical chronicler for the *New Annual Register,* a post he held until 1791. At this time Godwin dropped the title "reverend" from his name. This highly symbolic act may have been inspired by his conversations with the radical journalist, playwright, and novelist Thomas Holcroft (1745–1809), who was to become one of his closest friends. Other acquaintances of these early years in London include the poet Thomas Warton (1728–1790), the playwright Richard Brinsley Sheridan (1751–1816), the social reformer and abolitionist William Wilberforce (1759–1833), the philosopher John Horne Tooke (1736–1812), and Thomas Paine (1737–1809), author of *Rights of Man* (1791–92), which Godwin read in manuscript at the home of the wealthy philanthropist and radical dissenter Thomas Brand Hollis (1771–1805).

Godwin's best-known work, *Political Justice* (1793) was the product of several years of debate with his remarkable circle of friends as well as the concentrated study of ancient history and modern philosophy. Godwin received more than a thousand pounds—a princely sum for a work of its kind (£84,400 in 2021 terms)—for the copyright and initial printing of three hundred copies of this book. Although its high cost of three guineas was expected to restrict sales, *Political Justice* reached thousands of readers (mostly through the sharing of copies in lending libraries). The resulting celebrity catapulted Godwin into prominence as England's main spokesman for philosophical radicalism. For a brief period, he was one of the most famous people in Britain.

Books One and Two of *Political Justice* consider the social nature of humans and their origins. In Book Three Godwin provides an historical survey of the emergence of human governments. Book Four is concerned with the rights of the individual, which include the right to express dissent and to overthrow unjust governments. Godwin also argues in unity with Rousseau that human beings are naturally benevolent. Book Five includes a debate over the virtues of legislative versus executive government and concludes with a condemnation of all systems of government as essentially evil, since their function is to restrict the rights of individuals. In Book Six Godwin names those areas of life in danger of too much governmental interference, including religion, education, and the freedom of employment. Book Seven anticipates Michel Foucault's *To Discipline and Punish: The Birth of the Prison* (1975), arguing that punishment and constraint are the purest expressions of government and that crime must be considered wholly social in origin. In Book Eight private property is condemned as a fundamentally corrupt influence upon society, while marriage is denounced as a curtailment of individual freedom. Throughout *Political Justice* Godwin makes his points in a direct, lapidary style free from stylistic affectation, and his arguments remain consistent throughout: humans are essentially good; government is inescapably evil; vice, as Socrates teaches, is the product of imperfect knowledge. A permanent revolution will transform society as soon as reason is embraced by all humankind. Many of Godwin's positions anticipate the views of his daughter Mary and future son-in-law Percy Bysshe Shelley.

Despite the British government's suppression of dissent following France's declaration of war in 1793, Godwin was destined to have one more moment in the spotlight. In early autumn 1794, he reacted to the imprisonment and trial for high treason of his friend Holcroft, the ex-slave and writer Olaudah Equiano (1745–1797), and ten other members of the radical London Corresponding Society by publishing *Cursory Strictures on the Charge delivered by Lord Chief Justice Eyre to the Grand Jury, October 2, 1794*. This pamphlet, which includes some of Godwin's most trenchant writing, argues that the accused, who faced execution or exile in Australia if convicted, were unfairly charged with conspiracy to overthrow the government. Once again, this act of defiance succeeded, and the prisoners were released.

Godwin's next novel, *Things as They Are; or, the Adventures of Caleb Williams* (1794), far surpassed his previous fiction in imaginative power and psychological insight. Godwin described this remarkable work as "the offspring of that temper of mind in which the composition of my *Political Justice* left me."[5] The novel's compelling indictment of a social order founded on essential inequality and maintained by fear of persecution, which was ignited by the trial of his friends, can be felt in the preface to the 1795 edition: "Terror was the order of the day; and it was feared that even the humble novelist, might be shown to be constructively a traitor."[6] The terror to which he alluded is that experienced by the protagonist who is

---

5   Quoted in C. Kegan Paul, *William Godwin: His Friends and Contemporaries* (London: Henry S. King and Co., 1876), Vol. I, 78.

6   William Godwin, *Things As They Are; or, The Adventures of Caleb Williams*, 3 Volumes (London: Printed for B. Crosby, 1795). The preface, as Godwin explains, was withdrawn from the first edition "in compliance with the alarms of booksellers."

pursued by his erstwhile employer, Ferdinando Falkland, after Caleb discovers that Falkland has permitted innocent men take the blame for a murder he committed. Caleb's flight, eventual imprisonment and release result in radical disillusionment with the legal system, which is shown to be dominated by the ruling classes, whose chief representative is Falkland himself. The success of the novel exceeded even that of *Political Justice*, with three editions appearing before 1797, not including pirated foreign editions and translations. A stage version, entitled *The Iron Chest* (1796), was published by George Colman the Younger (1762–1836) and, even at a time of politically motivated censorship, was popular for decades.

Always gregarious and accustomed, even in the worst of times, to socializing, Godwin formed friendships with distinguished figures from all walks of life, including Thomas Wedgwood (1771–1805), Coleridge's patron, and the novelists Elizabeth Inchbald (1753–1821) and Maria Reveley Gisborne (1770–1836). Literary success afforded Godwin new opportunities to circulate in polite society. Always attracted to talented women of the day, such as Amelia Alderson Opie (1769–1853), Gisborne, and Inchbald, Godwin was taken with Mary Wollstonecraft when they met for the second time in 1796. At their first meeting, during a dinner for Thomas Paine, Godwin had felt that she was too strongly opinionated. As the author of *A Vindication of the Rights of Man* (1790) and *A Vindication of the Rights of Woman* (1792), Wollstonecraft was remarkably accomplished and the leading feminist of the age. She was, moreover, physically striking, and she made an additional claim on Godwin's sympathy: namely, her recent abandonment by Gilbert Imlay (1754–1828), businessman, U.S. ambassador to France, and father of her first child, Fanny. Before long, an attachment formed between them. Affection was strengthened by intellectual affinity, but they nonetheless remained steadfast in their philosophical opposition to marriage—until Wollstonecraft became pregnant in 1796. Despite his antipathy to the institution that he called "the most odious of all monopolies,"[7] Godwin acceded to her wishes that they marry and prevent the birth of another illegitimate child. Their marriage took place at Old St. Pancras Church on March 29, 1797. To avoid embarrassing their friends by what could be perceived as their act of hypocrisy, the couple initially occupied separate apartments. When news of the wedding became known, both Inchbald and Reveley expressed their disappointment.

The Godwins' daughter, Mary, was born on August 30, 1797, but Mary Wollstonecraft died of septicemia on September 10th. Her suffering was unspeakable and into the grief-stricken Godwin's care came their baby and Mary's daughter with Imlay to whom he gave the name Fanny Godwin. With meager financial resources and two small children to support, Godwin could not, despite his grief, afford to waste a moment. Seeking relief from his sorrow, he threw himself into editing his late wife's collected works and correspondence. In 1798 he published *Memoirs of the author of a Vindication of the Rights of Woman*, which is noteworthy, above all, for its candor and sensitivity in dealing with Wollstonecraft's troubled love affairs with Imlay and the Swiss painter and writer Henry Fuseli. Godwin also published a volume of familiar essays entitled *The Enquirer, Reflections on Education, Manners, and Literature* (1797), which was based on the template of *The Tatler* and *The Spectator* of Joseph Addison (1672–1719) and Richard Steele (1672–1729). One of the essays, "Of Avarice and Profusion," inspired Thomas Malthus (1766–1834) to compose, by way of reply, his famously pessimistic *Essay on the Principle of Population* (1798).

As if to counterbalance the tremendous outflow of discursive prose that kept his young children from starving, Godwin soon after published a new novel, *St. Leon: A Tale of the Sixteenth Century* (1798), which brought modest commercial success as well as praise from the critics. While noting in the *Edinburgh Review* that the plot lacked the "dramatic interest and intensity of purpose" of *Caleb*

---

7   *Political Justice*, 851.

Williams, William Hazlitt (1778–1830) argued that *St. Leon* is "set off by a more gorgeous and flowing eloquence, and by a crown of preternatural imagery, that waves over it like a palm tree." Godwin's versatility in writing polemical tracts and prose fiction reflects a mind neatly bifurcated between feeling and intellect, the impulse to create and the compulsion to analyze. Hazlitt describes this achievement as the result of supernatural intervention. Both kinds of writing "are as distinct as to style and subject matter, as if two different persons wrote them. No one in reading the philosophical treatise would suspect the embryonic romance: those who personally know Mr. Godwin would as little anticipate either . . . . It is as if a magician had produced some mighty feat of his art without warning." And as discordant as these two modes of writing seemed to many observers at the time, Hazlitt noted that "from the philosophical to the romantic visionary there was but one step."[8]

Objectified in the novels of Fyodor Dostoevsky (1821–1881) as either geographical exile or spiritual separation from others, the transgressor of social norms is fated to be punished by isolation, and in *St. Leon* the sense of isolation is heightened by Godwin's efforts to make the reader identify with his protagonist-narrator. This technique succeeds because of the author's thorough identification with Reginald. As Hazlitt puts it, "The work . . . and the author are one";[9] that is, the novel represents Godwin's attempt to dramatize the conflicts besetting his own existence. His personal life in ruins following the death of Mary Wollstonecraft, he found in the reactionary political climate, captured so effectively in the brooding atmosphere of *Caleb Williams*, that his professional fortunes were also wholly altered. Out of his sorrow at the loss of his wife, which was exacerbated both by his abandonment by friends and allies and the Sisyphean struggle to support his motherless daughters, Godwin

---

8   William Hazlitt, *The Spirit of the Age: Or Contemporary Portraits* (London: Henry Colburn, 1825), 46.

9   William Hazlitt, "Godwin," *Selections from the Edinburgh Review*, ed. Maurice Cross (Paris: Baudry's European Library, 1835), Vol. II, 444.

produced *St. Leon*. It was, in a sense, writing as compensatory ther-
apy. Godwin's literary art imitates life and thus redeems his existence from meaningless suffering. The protagonist of *St. Leon*, the
immortal possessor of the secret of the philosopher's stone, is the
alter ego of Godwin, the deeply flawed novelist. Both men are outlaws from society and both have been denied the kind of happiness
issuing from the "domestic affections." In addition, the alchemist's
art of turning base metals into gold corresponds to the novelist's
transmutation of life experience into symbolic form. Like Reginald,
the philosopher turned novelist is also a reluctant sorcerer, who has
been ostracized from human society on account of his magical powers—the alchemist because he cannot explain to anyone's satisfaction how he suddenly became rich; the philosopher because he
dared to confront the arbitrary power of the state with the divine
authority of reason. The philosopher's stone and *elixir vitae* are, finally, objective correlatives of the principles of *Political Justice*, and
the persecution inadvertently instigated by Reginald's displays of
benevolence throughout the novel suggests a recantation of this
same teaching.

P.N. Furbank suggests that *St. Leon* may be seen as Godwin's
"commentary upon his misfortunes," chief among these is the in-
cessant need for money to support a growing family. Godwin received three hundred pounds for the novel, an amount which
brought temporary relief from financial pressures.[10] But the author's difficulties only increased after 1797 as the forces of political
reaction rose up in response to the excesses of the Reign of Terror
in France (1793–1794) and the threat posed by the rise of Napoleon
Bonaparte in 1799. Godwin's once phenomenal popularity waned,
both among general readers and fashionable intellectuals. Signs of
change appeared in James Gillray's notorious caricature of Godwin,
Holcroft, and Paine; in Coleridge's attacks on *Political Justice* in his
lectures; and in Dr. Samuel Parr's attack on "the new philosophy"

---

10   P.N. Furbank, "Godwin's Novels," *Essays in Criticism* 5 (July 1955): 214–228.

in his *Spital Sermons* (1801). A parody, *St. Godwin: A Tale of the Six-teenth, Seventeenth, and Eighteenth Century*, which ridiculed God-win's writing and the melioristic views expressed in *St. Leon*, was published in 1800 by one Edward Dubois. Godwin's reply to Dr. Parr and other detractors, including the polymath James Mackin-tosh (1765–1832), and Malthus's *Thoughts. Occasioned by the Perusal of Dr. Parr's Spital Sermons*, appeared a year later. Godwin went fur-ther still to placate his old friends: he was reconciled with Coleridge after agreeing to soften his atheism who then introduced him to William Wordsworth (1770–1850) and the essayist Charles Lamb (1775–1834).

Godwin's reading during this period embraced the major Eng-lish playwrights, and Lamb and Coleridge helped arrange for his imitation of Elizabethan drama, *Antonio*, to be produced at the The-atre Royal, Drury Lane, on December 13, 1800. The play, however, proved a financial failure. Undeterred, Godwin, at Coleridge's urg-ing, undertook a biography and social history of Chaucer and his age. After more than two years of unremitting labor, much of it con-sisting of original archival research in the British Museum, the *Life of Geoffrey Chaucer* appeared in two volumes in October 1803, for which Godwin received six hundred pounds.

In December 1801 Godwin married for a second time. Mary Jane Clairmont was a widow with a son, Charles, and a daughter, Jane, who later changed her name to Claire. Mrs. Clairmont had come to live in the same neighborhood and introduced herself to Godwin by asking, "Is it possible that I behold the immortal God-win?" They entered into an amicable but, it is reported, passionless marriage of convenience, which produced one child, William God-win, Jr., who was born on March 28, 1803. (He died in September 1832 after attaining a modest reputation as a writer.) A growing family and concomitant financial pressures forced Godwin and his new wife to embark on a new venture, a combined bookbindery and bookshop, which was typical of the vertical integration of the publishing industry at this time. The Juvenile Library, which specialized in grammars, histories, school texts, and children's books, was the focus of their efforts. The political disfavor with which the name of Godwin was greeted in London forced William to publish under a collection of pseudonyms, including Edward Baldwin and the exotic Theophilus Marcliffe. Examples of the works he published in this period include *Fables, Ancient and Modern. Adapted for the Use of Children* (1805), *The Life of Lady Jane Grey* (1806), *The History of England, For the Use of Schools and Young Persons* (1806), and *The History of Rome: From the Building of the City to the Ruin of the Republic* (1809). Of the many commissions solicited by The Juvenile Library, one work was an instant classic, Charles and Mary Lamb's *Tales from Shakespear* (1807). But such successes were few and the Godwins' publishing house continuously teetered on the brink of financial ruin. Godwin acquired his reputation as an inveterate borrower during these years.

In January 1811 the first letter addressed to Godwin from Percy Shelley arrived in which the young poet professes his great sense of obligation to the indigent philosopher and with it the promise of financial salvation. The protégé and mentor meet for the first time in October 1812. Thereafter, Shelley was a frequent visitor in the Godwin house on Skinner Street where he became acquainted with Mary Godwin. The following July, Shelley and Mary eloped to France and Switzerland, taking with them Mary's stepsister Claire, who had, in the meantime, become Byron's mistress. At the time the ménage took flight, Shelley was still married to his first wife, Harriet Westbrook (1795–1816), who was then pregnant with their third child. Her despair at being abandoned led to her suicide in November 1816. On October 9th of the same year Mary's half-sister Fanny Godwin poisoned herself with laudanum while on a visit to her deceased mother's sisters in Swansea, Wales.

Buffeted by financial strain and personal tragedy, Godwin persevered with his writing and published four major novels after *St. Leon*, including *Fleetwood: or, The New Man of Feeling* (1805). The protagonist, Casimir Fleetwood, is a misanthropic, dissolute, world-weary "new man of feeling," who travels around Europe in search of experiences that will reconcile him to life. Godwin's narrative is a "record" of Fleetwood's errors and his great act of contrition and humiliation.

Mandeville. A Tale of the Seventeenth Century in England, an historical novel that chronicles the English Civil War, was published in 1817. Charles Mandeville escapes the 1641 Irish Uprising with help from his wet nurse. He is educated at home by the Reverend Hilkiah Bradford and thereafter at Winchester and Oxford. He leaves Oxford briefly to serve the Royalist cause and is thwarted in his ambition to become secretary to Sir Joseph Wagstaff by his schoolfellow Lionel Clifford. Back at Oxford, another schoolmate, Mallison, viciously spreads rumors that Mandeville was either dismissed from the army or had deserted. Mandeville's resulting alienation from his fellow students hastens the growth of his misanthropy, a persistent element in his personality that was relieved only in the company of his beloved sister, Henrietta. Mandeville, however, is enraged when he receives word that Henrietta and Clifford are to be wed. His answer is to hire mercenaries to assist him in ambushing Clifford, Henrietta, and their party. In the fighting that follows, Mandeville receives a disfiguring wound that permanently distorts his mouth into a hideous grimace that objectifies his disgust for mankind.

The public greeted *Cloudesley: A Tale* (1830), with enthusiasm and the novel went into multiple editions. Its narrator, William Meadows, is a picaresque adventurer who, upon his father's death, is sent to sea. His travels take him from Britain to Russia, where, after a stint on the faculty of the University of St. Petersburg, he enters the service of John Earnest Biren, a confidential adviser to the Tsarina Anne. Meadows's intimacy with Isabella Schebatoff, Biren's niece, incurs the wrath of the Tsarina and he must beat a hasty escape to England via Amsterdam. Back in his native land, Meadows is summoned to the estate of Richard, Lord Danvers, which is located not far from his sister's farm. After hearing Meadows describe his ordeal in Russia, Lord Danvers confides in him the story of his life: how years ago he stole his nephew Julian's inheritance. He sends Meadows to Italy to find Julian and make amends. In a flashback, Cloudesley is revealed to be the son of a peasant on the Danvers estate at Milwood Park. Cloudesley enters Danvers's service after the nobleman saves him from prison. His chameleon-like change in character—from a grateful and utterly faithful servant to a greedy, vengeful egoist—occurs after he agrees to become the infant Julian's foster father. Years pass, and Julian joins a band of outlaws while Cloudesley goes to Ireland to see Lord Danvers. Upon his return, Cloudesley searches for Julian, stumbles into an ambush of mountain bandits, and is killed. Meadows later saves Julian from execution, and informs him of his heritage, at Danvers's behest.

Godwin finished his final novel in 1833, within three years of his death. *Deloraine* is the portrait of an arch-romantic outcast from society, a modern Cain, who offers this work as a confidential memoir. Deloraine describes how from birth to age forty he enjoyed all the privileges of the ruling class. He was elected to Parliament at age twenty-two and later served as ambassador from the English court to various governments on the Continent. His fortunes change, however, with the death of his exemplary first wife, the former Emilia Fitzcharles. Deloraine becomes ill and, during his convalescence in the north of England, he meets and then marries the hauntingly beautiful Margaret Borradale. Deloraine then learns that William, her true love, who had been presumed lost at sea, has miraculously survived, but he selfishly keeps this news to himself. When he returns home from a journey and discovers Margaret and William together, Deloraine flies into a rage and kills William. Margaret responds by dying of a stroke. Deloraine flees to the Continent with Catherine, his devoted daughter from his marriage to Emilia, with stops in Bruges, Ghent, and then to a solitary castle on the Rhine whose sole occupant is the mysterious Jerome. Deloraine and Catherine are hotly pursued by William's best friend, Travers, and they are forced to return to England where they take refuge on the estate belonging to Thornton, a trusted friend, who then accompanies them into permanent exile in Holland.

Besides the aforementioned novels, Godwin's latter years saw the publication of a monumental *History of the Commonwealth of England* (1824–1828). Predictably radical in its sympathies, Godwin's *History* is noteworthy in its scholarly treatment of the period. This work anticipates *Oliver Cromwell's Letters and Speeches* (1845–1846) published by Thomas Carlyle (1795–1881) in its sympathetic portrayal of the anti-royalist Lord Protector. In 1833 George, Earl Grey (1767–1828), responding to the recommendations of Mackintosh and other friends, appointed Godwin to a lifelong sinecure in the Office of the Exchequer. Godwin's last written work, besides essays that were collected and published as *Essays Never Before Published* (1873), was *Lives of the Necromancers* (1834), a return to the exploration of the supernatural in *St. Leon*.

Godwin succumbed to the complications of a winter cold on April 7, 1836. In accordance with his will, he was buried next to Mary Wollstonecraft in the Old St. Pancras churchyard. In 1851 the remains of Godwin and Wollstonecraft were joined with Mary Shelley's and the casket bearing Percy Shelley's heart at St. Peter's churchyard in Bournemouth. The second Mrs. Godwin, Mary Jane, died on June 17, 1841.

To historians and critics of English culture during the long Romantic Period, William Godwin is seen in many guises. To his young followers among the Romantic poets and writers, he was, as author of *Political Justice* (1793), deeply influential as a proponent of the struggle for liberty that began with the fall of the Bastille. To a broader readership, Godwin was best known as the author of the highly regarded novel *Caleb Williams* (1794), whose alternate title, *Things as They Are*, suggests that this stirring narrative also embodies a critique of England's social and legal systems. To his many creditors and long-suffering friends, Godwin was an impecunious, debt-ridden bookseller, editor, and author who was forced because of political persecution to publish a myriad of works under pseu-donyms. He borrowed money from one and all, including, in one instance related in the diary of Crabb Robinson, a total stranger. And only ten years after his death, as Thomas De Quincey (1785–1859) noted, Godwin was clearly remembered "less by the novels that succeeded, or by the philosophy that he abjured than as the man that had Mary Wollstonecraft for his wife, Mary Shelley for his daughter, and the immortal Shelley as his son-in-law."[11] While Godwin's reputation as philosopher faded over the years, it was nonetheless as a philosopher that, in De Quincey's words, "he car-ried one single shock into the bosom of English society, fearful but momentary, like that from the electric blow of the [South American electric fish] gymnotus."[12]

The popular image of Godwin has done little to discourage a lopsided estimate of his literary output. The portrait of the portly, slightly hunched Skinner Street bookdealer—to whose fall from lit-erary eminence was added the scent of scandal brought on by his publication of the remarkably candid *Memoirs of the Author of a Vin-dication of the Rights of Woman* (1798) and more than a suggestion of impropriety in his haggling with Shelley over money—is at vari-ance with the energetic, intellectually courageous figure of his youth. Godwin's best work, it is true, was written before 1799; his writing after this is less accessible—the novels elude easy classifi-cation; their style is looser and their plots are labyrinthine. Moreo-ver, Godwin made the risky decision to abandon the successful for-mula that brought him fame with *Caleb Williams*—a tale of unjust persecution and pursuit which is a subgenre of the Gothic novel. By the time of Mary Godwin's elopement with Shelley, Godwin seemed, at best, a relic of the generation of 1789 and, at worst, one who had compromised his own philosophical legacy by taking

---

11   Thomas De Quincey, "Notes on Gilfillans' Literary Portraits: William Godwin (1859)," in *De Quincey's Collected Writings*, 14 Volumes, ed. David Masson (E-dinburgh: Adam & Charles Black, 1890), Vol. XI, 335.

12   *Ibid.*, 327.

money from Shelley, apparently in exchange for his daughter and stepdaughter.

Sic gloria transit mundi — the eclipse of a once bright star in the intellectual firmament — is also the theme of William Hazlitt's contemporary portrait of Godwin in *The Spirit of the Age* (1825), which begins with a discussion of *Political Justice*. Godwin's book ignited English public opinion, which had been previously rendered combustible by the thrilling rhetoric in competing pamphlets published by Edmund Burke (1729–1797), *Reflections on the Revolution in France* (1790), and Thomas Paine (1737–1809), *The Rights of Man* (1791). Godwin's optimistic "utilitarian" doctrine (first described as such by Hazlitt) trusts in innate human goodness and identifies sincerity as the vehicle of a peaceful revolution that will transform society by sweeping away injustice. This doctrine seems to give voice to the ethical conscience and to delimit the political ambitions of the Romantic generation. The ideological kernel of the work is found in Book Four, Chapter 4: "If every man today would tell all the truth he knows, three years hence there would be scarcely a falsehood of any magnitude remaining in the civilized world." The success of *Political Justice* plucked Godwin from obscurity. He was lionized in Whig drawing rooms and acclaimed a benevolent genius by an unusual coalition of writers, Oxford and Cambridge dons, and intellectually ambitious schoolboys. The ardor felt by Godwin's admirers is captured in a sonnet Coleridge sent to Robert Southey in December 1794. Although he had yet to read *Political Justice*, Coleridge praises Godwin as a savor bringing light to a dark world:

> O form'd t'illumine a sunless world forlorn,
>   As o'er the chill and dusky brow of Night,
>   In Finland's wintry skies the Mimic Morn
> Electric pours a stream of rosy light,
> Pleas'd I have mark'd OPPRESSION, terror-pale,
>   Since, thro' the windings of her dark machine,
>   Thy steady eye has shot its glances keen —
> And bade th' All-lovely "scenes at distance hail."
> Nor will I not thy holy guidance bless,

> And hymn thee, GODWIN! with an ardent lay;
>   For that thy voice, in Passions' stormy day,
> When wild I roam'd the bleak Heath of Distress,
> Bade the bright form of Justice meet thy way—
> And told me that her name was HAPPINESS.

Indeed, as Hazlitt observes, in the revolutionary atmosphere of *fin-de-siécle* England, "no one was more talked of, more looked up to, more sought after" than Godwin. And "no work" at that time "gave such a blow to the philosophical mind of the country as the celebrated *Enquiry concerning Political Justice*. Tom Paine was considered for a time as a Tom Fool to him; [William] Paley an old woman; Edmund Burke a flashy sophist."[13] Although the influence of this treatise followed the ephemeral trajectory of a Roman candle, even Wordsworth—who was capable of being unresponsive to a writer as electrifying to others as Johann Wolfgang von Goethe (1749–1832)—enthused over Godwin and once advised a young student to "throw aside" his chemistry books for Godwin's writings on necessity. Moreover, Godwin's charismatic optimism heavily influenced Hazlitt in the years 1798–1805, the period in which he wrote *An Essay on the Principles of Human Action* (1805), and Hazlitt's generation as a whole recognized in Godwin "another Prospero" who "uttered syllables that with their enchanted breath were to change the world, and might almost stop the stars in their courses." But, if for Hazlitt, the "Spirit of the Age was never more fully shown than in its treatment of this writer—its love of paradox and change, its dastard submissions to prejudice and to the fashion of the day,"[14] it was also symptomatic of the fickleness of the times that Godwin the philosopher should have surprised his contemporaries by an unexpected metamorphosis into a popular novelist. Their admiration only increased when the chameleonic nature of his achievement was fully recognized. Before the publication of either Coleridge's *Biographia Literaria* (1817) or Shelley's philosophical poems, when

---

13   Hazlitt, *Spirit of the Age*, 30.
14   *Ibid.*, 29.

English critics were unfavorably disposed to the fusion of philosophy and poetry that distinguishes German Classicism and Romanticism, it was generally held that "the poetic and metaphysical tem-
peraments" were, in Leslie Stephen's phrase, "in some sense incompatible."[15] The appearance, then, of two highly successful novels—
Caleb Williams in 1794 and *St. Leon* in 1799—gave Godwin's followers an additional, unforeseen justification for their high estimate of
his talents, and his critics a new arrow for their quiver.

If Godwin's Romantic critics are deferential and respectful as
befits an admired sage and teacher of a generation of writers who
reached maturity in the shadow of the French Revolution, the Victorian reevaluation of his standing is far less generous. The memory
of his youthful assault on the English establishment was blotted out
by an emphasis on his financial difficulties and personal foibles.
Later nineteenth-century critics seem to focus obsessively on these,
leaving it to historians of the future to arrive at a more balanced
judgment of his life and literary achievements. Leslie Stephen's article in the *Dictionary of National Biography* is typical of the Victorian
approach to Godwin in its ad hominem argument. Stephen homes
in on the inconsistency between Godwin's professed opposition to
the institution of marriage as found in the first edition of *Political
Justice* but "neutralized" in subsequent editions, and his highly
equivocal behavior following Mary Godwin's elopement with Shelley. Although he was so enraged with Shelley that he "refused to
communicate" with him "except through his solicitors, and forbade
Fanny Godwin to speak to her sister," he "was not above taking
1000 pounds from Shelley and begging for more. Godwin, constantly sinking into deeper embarrassment, tried to extort money
from his son-in-law until Shelley's death, and Shelley did his best
to supply the venerable horseleech."[16] Such transparent para-

---

15   Leslie Stephen, "Godwin and Shelley," *Hours in a Library* (New York and Lon-
      don: G.P. Putnam's Sons, 1899), Vol. III, 64.
16   Leslie Stephen, "Godwin," *Dictionary of National Biography*, ed. Leslie Stephen
      and Sidney Lee (London: Smith, Elder & Co., 1890), Vol. XXII, 67.

sitism—coupled with the perception of intellectual inconsistency that less charitable commentators condemned as hypocrisy—only revived the chorus of criticism that was first heard when Godwin published his unblushing revelations of Mary Wollstonecraft's liaison with Gilbert Imlay in *Memoirs of the Author of the Vindication of the Rights of Woman*. Torn between financial need and somehow restoring his shattered self-respect, Godwin's vacillations permanently damaged his reputation. And although the Romantic generation included other "outlaws" and transgressors of moral norms, the sins of Coleridge, Byron, and De Quincey were perceived as venial in comparison with Godwin's apparent sale of his daughter to Shelley, or were—in the way that Byron's honorable death in Greece saved his name for posterity—redeemed in later life. Stephen's tone of moral censure seems to come straight out of articles penned by Godwin's conservative critics in a Tory journal such as the *Anti-Jacobin Review*. However, Godwin's venal behavior toward Shelley does confirm a pattern of borrowing accompanied by the unflattering rationalization that, as one of the philosophical saviors of humankind, he felt he deserved assistance from others who were better off than he. Godwin seemed psychologically equipped to cope with rejection and poverty because of his pride in the authorship of *Political Justice* and his austere apprenticeship as a dissenting minister. He escaped the fate of the artist and diarist Benjamin Robert Haydon (1786–1846)—who was similarly burdened by a large family and driven to suicide by professional failure—owing to an improbable patron, His Majesty's government, which rewarded its onetime adversary with a sinecure in the Office of the Exchequer.

In the third volume of *Studies of a Biographer* (1902) Stephen approaches *Caleb Williams*, Godwin's masterpiece, as a direct offshoot of *Political Justice*. The philosophical conviction that gives *Political Justice* its vehemence also sustains the novel's extraordinary atmosphere of fear and anxiety, making it "a kind of literary curiosity—a monstrous hybrid between different species . . . the kind of text which might have been treated effectively in the old moral tale of the *Candide* variety." That *Caleb Williams* "can be read without the pressure of a sense of duty" is undeniable, but it owes its interest to the "good luck that his philosophy provided him with an effective situation."[17] In *Hours in a Library* (1904) Stephen examines the relationship between Godwin and Percy Shelley, which was famously initiated by the young poet. Stephen notes that at each stage in Shelley's career, the influence of Godwin is palpable, from "the crude poetry of *Queen Mab*, where many passages read like the *Political Justice* done into verse" to his accomplished performances as a poet, since "even in the *Prometheus* and his last writings we find a continued reflection of Godwin's characteristic views."[18]

For the late nineteenth century, Stephen's moralistic stance held sway as critical orthodoxy. But signs of Godwin's critical rehabilitation appeared with the publication of Charles Kegan Paul's *William Godwin: His Friends and Contemporaries* (1876) and H.N. Brailsford's *Shelley, Godwin, and Their Circle* (1913). Both books set out to define Godwin's role as a leader in the intellectual life of the Romantic era. This approach to Godwin's life and work as a matrix of creativity and influence was effectively revived in William St. Clair's *The Godwins and the Shelleys* (1989). The first full-scale twentieth-century biography was Ford K. Brown's *The Life of William Godwin* (1926). Within a decade or two, rehabilitation was followed by adulation, as Godwin's philosophical writings were found to support a variety of radical causes, from anarchism and pacifism to vegetarianism and state socialism. Anarchists considered him an important precursor to Karl Marx (1818–1883), Pierre-Joseph Proudhon (1809–1865), Mikhail Bakunin (1814–1876), and Peter Kropotkin (1842–1921), and efforts were made to depict him as a political prophet rather than a mere man of letters. George Woodcock's *William Godwin: A Biographical Sketch* (1946) first suggests this connection to anarchism.

---

17   Leslie Stephen, "William Godwin's Novels," *Studies of a Biographer*, second series (London: G.P. Putnam's Sons, 1907), Vol. III, 143.
18   Stephens, "Godwin and Shelley," *Hours in a Library*, 79.

Since the end of World War Two, Godwin's critics have tended to assume a neutral or disinterested position toward his political views as if they formed the belief system of some quaint or primitive sect, but they continue to subject his life and writings to analysis and interpretation. Successors to Brown's 1926 biography include studies by David Fleisher (1951) and Don Locke (1980). The best short work that combines biography with an interpretation of the major works is Elton Edward Smith and Esther Greenwood Smith's volume in the Twayne series (1965). Starting in the 1950s Godwin's later novels began to receive due attention. Previously dismissed as mere potboilers or the embarrassing efforts of a writer well past his prime, these novels only began to receive serious attention with the appearance of articles and books by P.N. Furbank (1955), George Sherburn (1962), Wallace A. Flanders (1967), Robert D. Hume (1969), David McCracken (1970), Dean T. Hughes (1980), and Peter H. Marshall (1984). These critics share a concern with reading the late novels as canonical elements in Godwin's oeuvre. A great deal of work remains to be done on Godwin's miscellaneous prose—his biography of Chaucer, his histories of England and Rome, his myriad political pamphlets, and children's books—to assess the literary and historical value of this varied material and its relationship to his acknowledged masterpieces and his life experience.

7 German Literature and English Radicalism

> "As wine and oil are imported to us from abroad, so must ripe understanding, and many civic virtues, be imported into our minds from foreign writings; — we shall else miscarry still, and come short in the attempt of any great enterprise."
>
> John Milton, *History of Britain* (1670)

The essential bond between the transmission of German culture in Britain and the emergence of leading voices of Dissent, radical politics, and feminism in the late eighteenth century has not yet been fully articulated.[1] Similarly, what has also not been fully acknowledged is the prosthetic ligature between the translation and criticism of German literature, on the one hand, and the appearance of original works by radical authors, on the other. Thomas Holcroft and William Taylor's efforts as intermediaries between British and German culture throw into sharp relief the reciprocal relationship between the mediation of German culture in Britain and the rise of Jacobinism—Romanticism in process—that we find on the margins of mainstream British literary culture. While Holcroft's novels have received a good deal of scholarly attention,[2] his achievement as a

---

1   The scholarship on the transmission of German culture in late eighteenth-century England is limited. One of the earliest authoritative investigations of this specific relationship is John Boening's article, "Pioneers and Precedents: The 'Importation of German' and the Emergence of Periodical Criticism in England," *Internationales Archiv für Sozialgeschichte der deutschen Literatur* VII (1982): 65–87. The emphasis in Boening's article is on the innovative character of William Taylor's career as a reviewer for *The Monthly Review* and on the emergence of a class of professional literary critics in England that can be traced to the criticism of German literature in the reviews.

2   See especially Miriam L. Wallace, *Revolutionary Subjects in the English 'Jacobin' Novel, 1790–1805* (Lewisburg: Bucknell University Press, 2009); Allene Gregory, *The French Revolution and the English Novel* (New York and London: G.P. Putnam's Sons, 1915); C.B.A. Proper, *Social Elements in English Prose Fiction between 1771–1832* (New York: Haskell House, 1965 [1929]); Virgil R. Stallbaumer, "Thomas Holcroft as a Novelist," *ELH* XV (1948): 194–218; J. M. S. Thompkins,

transmitter of German culture has been largely overshadowed by the work of more prominent intermediaries among the radical *habitués* of Joseph Johnson's bookshop—Henry Fuseli and Mary Wollstonecraft—all of whom were associated with William Godwin in one way or another. For instance, Godwin shared Taylor's upbringing in a Dissenting household and Norwich roots; Holcroft was his best friend, Wollstonecraft was his wife, and, in addition to friends, he shared with Fuseli the experience of having originally trained for the clergy. But on account of the scope of his translations—what he called "this just and necessary sufferance"[3]—which included the work of such major figures as Goethe, Johann Kaspar Lavater (1741–1801), Friedrich II (Frederick the Great) (1721–1786), and Friedrich Leopold Graf zu Stolberg-Stolberg (1750–1819) in travel writing, poetry, memoirs, and plays—the case of Holcroft discloses to a greater degree the connections between the transmission of German culture and radical politics in Britain.[4]

An examination of this affinity reveals that the turn to German literature among proponents of radical reform answered a deep-seated need in the culture of political and religious Dissent for a

---

The Popular Novel in England, 1770–1800 (Lincoln and London: University of Nebraska Press, 1961); Rodney M. Baine, *Thomas Holcroft and the Revolutionary Novel* (Athens: University of Georgia Press, 1965); and Gary Kelly, *The English Jacobin Novel 1780–1805* (Oxford: The Clarendon Press, 1976). For details on Holcroft's biography the main sources are *The Memoirs of the late Thomas Holcroft* (completed in 1810 and published in 1816) in *The Complete Works of William Hazlitt*, ed. P. P. Howe (London: J. M. Dent & Sons Ltd., 1932; rpt., New York: AMS Press, 1967); Charles Kegan Paul's *William Godwin: His Friends and Contemporaries* (London: Henry S. King & Co., 1876); and *Letters of Charles Lamb*, ed. Alfred Ainger (London: Macmillan and Co., 1888).

3   Preface to Frederic Leopold Count Stolberg, *Travels through Germany, Switzerland, Italy, and Sicily*, trans. Thomas Holcroft (London: G. G. J. and J. Robinson, 1796), Vol. I, iv.

4   Evidence of the affinity between German literature and radicalism is seen in Godwin's interest in *Werther* (which he was reading at the time of Wollstonecraft's death), in Mary Shelley's inclusion of Goethe's novel among the books read by Victor Frankenstein's monstrous autodidact, in P. B. Shelley's fragmentary translation of *Faust*, and in Coleridge's intense engagement with German culture as revealed in *Biographia Literaria* (1817).

breakthrough from insularity into cosmopolitanism, for growth and development achieved along an axis of confrontation between the familiar and the foreign, the self and the other. The response to German culture as an opening up to otherness and an alternative to native sources of self-formation emerged as an ideological litmus test for radical or reform-minded intellectuals seeking access to British literary and academic institutions.[5] The texts generated as a response to German culture—translations and criticism—must be seen as acts of interpretation that inevitably encode authorial biases reflecting political, class, generational, and religious identities. For English radicals the appropriation of German culture replaced the Oxbridge or public school education based on Latin and Greek that had been denied them on account of gender, class or religion. While the identification of spiritual growth with the study of German culture is inseparable from the quest for cultural authority, the attraction of German culture also consisted in its scientific-critical orientation and a dynamic configuration of humanism based on historicity, psychology, and subjective emotion that contrasted with more static characterizations of human nature, perception, and experience associated with the Enlightenment. Embracing review criticism and biography, translations and compilations (of *belles lettres* as well as scientific and philosophical tracts, history and biography), loose adaptations and instances of outright plagiarism, the texts transmitted comprise a diverse body of literary activity that made German texts accessible through modification by such contingent qualities as taste, idiosyncrasy, and even inaccurate or misleading interpretations. As women, dissenters, radicals, and other members of culturally dispossessed groups, the writers involved in the transmission of German culture at this time occupied the periphery of mainstream literary circles in Britain and their

---

5   For an example from the early nineteenth century, in 1828 Carlyle applied for appointment to a professorship at St. Andrew's University on the strength of his reviews and translations of German literature; in fact, Goethe served as one of Carlyle's referees.

ideological preoccupations (sympathy with the aims of the French Revolution, the expansion of the voting franchise, legal and economic reform, and the removal of social and political barriers to dissenters and women) are reflected in their mediation activities.

The "domestication" of German culture was, for Holcroft, a means of acquiring cultural capital from an indifferent, even hostile dominant culture and its publishing institutions—booksellers, rival authors, journal and newspaper editors, government censors, and the reading public formed by them—by creating independent institutions in a kind of dissident parallel universe. Translating Goethe and his contemporaries in Germany thus served as an empowering platform for the assertion of an alternative set of political and aesthetic values that challenged the standard paradigm. Reviewing and translating German authors offered a prototype of literary development according to which mediators became original writers following an apprenticeship of translation and reviewing. Indeed, ventriloquizing or "re-writing" is a vehicle that facilitates original writing, and for the generation of 1789 in Britain conscious imitation is a key stage in the process by which literary identity is formed. At the same time the texts that were produced as an expression of Goethean emulation serve as forms of indirect but nonetheless subversive self-expression. Official censors and compliantly self-censoring booksellers and publishers tolerated levels of "subversion" in translated foreign works that would not have been acceptable in English language original books. And texts associated with political radicalism were also invariably deemed aesthetically and ethically transgressive. The emergence in late eighteenth-century Britain of hermeneutic vehicles for the transmission of German culture may be likened to what André Malraux in *Les voix du silence* [*The Voices of Silence*] (1951) termed a "conquest," an "annexation," and a "possession" of otherness and it is certainly a crucial period in the history of British culture when the interpretation and transmission of a foreign literary tradition takes on political and cultural significance. Translating and reviewing German texts was, for

Holcroft and Taylor, an expression of sympathy for the aims of the French Revolution as well as the experience of inner emigration and political marginalization.[6]

The social, political, fictive, and mediative writings of English radicals replicate an intricate web of interrelated and interdependent voices, a region of the mind which is situated on the margins of all these disciplines, at their junctures and points of intersection. Entering this polyphonic borderland we are in an advantageous position from which to approach Holcroft and Taylor's literary careers, especially their contributions to the transmission of German culture in Britain. Dismissed even by many recent critics as the creator of a minor sub-genre, "novels of purpose," perhaps in order to distinguish his work from the less overtly ideological novels of the canon, Holcroft's best novels—*Anna St. Ives* (1792) and *Hugh Trevor* (begun in 1794)—had either appeared or were well under way at the time of his arrest in 1794. However subversively one might read canonical Gothic novels such as Ann Radcliffe's *The Mysteries of Udolpho* (1794) and M.G. Lewis's *The Monk* (1796), Holcroft's novels unabashedly espouse a radical political agenda. For Holcroft fictional discourse was merely another means of giving voice to the ideological struggle taking place between monarchist Britain and revolutionary France. Employing the black and white ideological palette of propaganda literature, his protagonists persistently advocate the adoption of a new moral code and predict the inevitable triumph of a revolutionary social and political program that will reeducate and thus recreate the human race along wholly new lines. Published a few months before Godwin's *An Enquiry Concerning Political Justice* (1793), *Anna St. Ives* anticipates in detail many of the arguments presented in Godwin's widely influential treatise, a coincidence explained in large part by the daily discussions between the two writers that took place as both works were in progress. As

---

6   See James Simpson, *"The Authority of Culture*: Some Reflections on the Reception of a Classic," in *Goethe and the English-Speaking World*, 185–198.

Godwin put it in a letter to Hazlitt, "the principles afterwards developed in my *Political Justice* were the almost constant topic of conversation between Holcroft and myself."[7]

Identified by Godwin as one of his four principle "oral educators,"[8] Holcroft's worldview was largely shaped by the leading writers of Continental Deism—Antoine François Prévost (1697–1763), Jean-Jacques Rousseau (1712–1778), Denis Diderot (1713–1784), Louis-Sébastien Mercier (1740–1814), Christoph Martin Wieland (1733–1813), and, of course, Voltaire (1694–1778)—and he is chiefly remembered today as one of the twelve British radicals who were indicted for high treason in 1794. This group, which included John Horne Tooke (1736–1812) and Thomas Hardy (1736–1832), a shoemaker, an autodidact like Holcroft, and founder of the London Corresponding Society in 1792, was swept up in the government's campaign to eviscerate the reform movement, a process that began with the trial and conviction—in absentia—of Thomas Paine (1737–1809) for seditious libel in 1792. It is interesting to note that Godwin's suppressed preface to the original edition of *Caleb Williams*, in which he declares emphatically that it is a novel about injustice, is in fact dated the day of Hardy's arrest, May 12, 1794. As he remarks in a note appended to the second edition published in 1795: "terror was the order of the day; and it was feared that even the humble novelist might be shown to be constructively a traitor."[9] Godwin's response to the arrest of his colleagues in the reform movement did not end with his examination of "Things As They Are" with respect to "the modes of domestic and unrecorded

---

7   Charles Kegan Paul, *William Godwin: His Friends and Contemporaries*, Vol. I, 64–65.

8   Charles Kegan Paul, *William Godwin: His Friends and Contemporaries*, Vol. I, 357: "In my 31st year [1787] I became acquainted with Mr. Thomas Holcroft, and it was probably in consequence of our mutual conversations that I became two years after an unbeliever, and in my 36th year an atheist."

9   William Godwin, *Things as They Are; or, the Adventures of Caleb Williams*, ed. and intro. Maurice Hindle (Hammondsworth: Penguin Books, 1988), 4.

despotism by which man becomes the destroyer of man."[10] Demonstrating unexpected nimbleness for a mind unfairly seen by posterity as somewhat plodding and discursive rather than agile and intuitive, Godwin turned from allegorical treatment of the government's monopoly of power in *Caleb Williams* to direct confrontation with the judicial system in a heroic feat of political journalism. Without accepting his claim to the lion's share of the credit for the full acquittal of Hardy, Tooke, and Holcroft, we still might agree with Marilyn Butler that the public outcry that greeted Godwin's pamphlet, *Cursory Strictures on the Charge Delivered by Lord Chief Justice Eyre to the Grand Jury, October 2, 1794*, was evidence that "the defence of liberty could still, given the occasion and the rhetorician, outweigh fears for property, and muster in the opposition some sense of a common cause."[11]

Holcroft evaded the hangman's noose and transportation to Australia's Botany Bay—the fate of those convicted of treason—only to endure the figurative death of his literary voice in the ensuing years of unrelenting political repression and media censorship. Indeed, his declining fortunes as a playwright paralleled the trajectory of the public's decreasing appetite for ideological theater with its *de rigueur* attacks on established authority and upper class privilege. An example of the social criticism to which theater audiences suddenly reacted with howls and catcalls is found in the following speech (in Act V, Scene 4) by the protagonist in Holcroft's drama *Love's Frailties* (1794): "I was bred to the most useless and often the most worthless of all professions; that of a gentleman."[12] If Holcroft and his fellow advocates of reform were to remain faithful to their "religion" as defined in *The Rights of Man* as "do[ing] good," the price paid for such altruism was growing cultural marginalization.

---

10   William Godwin, *Caleb Williams*, 3.
11   Marilyn Butler, ed., *Burke, Paine, Godwin, and the Revolution Controversy* (Cambridge: Cambridge University Press, 1989), 170.
12   Thomas Holcroft, *Love's Frailties* (Covent Garden: Shepperson and Reynolds, 1794), 29.

Denied access to the booksellers and theater managers who had previously published and produced his novels and plays, Holcroft turned to translation for the second time in his career, albeit with greater urgency than before. Half a dozen years earlier, following his first trip to France, where he was befriended by the revolutionary journalist Nicholas Bonneville (1760–1828) and the dramatist Louis-Sébastien Mercier (1740–1814), Holcroft had translated a number of texts, including Pierre Beaumarchais's *The Marriage of Figaro* (1785), several novels by the Madame de Genlis (1746–1830), and the *Posthumous Works of Frederick the Great* (13 volumes, 1789) which he translated from the first French edition. The profits earned from this work allowed Holcroft to retire permanently from the stage where, according to accounts of fellow actors, he had displayed at best an indifferent talent. This phase of translation coincided, of course, with an upsurge in public interest and demand for foreign texts and Holcroft's work at this time was undertaken with no higher motive than to boil the pot as he sought to reestablish himself as a writer of original texts. For obvious reasons, however, the market for French literature declined in the later 1790s and Holcroft was forced to find an alternate source for texts to translate. This new source he would find in German literature — partly as a result of contact with and encouragement received from the dramatist Friedrich Gottlieb Klopstock (1724–1803), the Homeric translator Johann Heinrich Voss (1751–1826), the traveler Stolberg, and other prominent liberal German writers whom he met while living in political exile. But this time around financial pressure, while still a factor in his decision, was not the driving force behind his turn to the translation of German texts. Isolated from the cultural institutions and the literary marketplace that owed their existence to the state's sufferance or support, his career as a writer, his sense of identity and his economic security, followed the same trajectory as that of his fellow Jacobins and reformers. Translation, therefore, became Holcroft's chief creative and ideological outlet during the period of exile and cultural isolation from 1799–1803.

Prior to the treason trial in 1794 and the suppression of reform activity, Holcroft had been a prolific and a fairly successful author of comedies, light opera, and other pieces for the stage that regularly ran at Covent Garden. His greatest successes—pieces that ran into several editions—were, like his imitation of Beaumarchais's *Figaro*, often adaptations of French and German works and include plays with such titles as *The School for Arrogance* (two editions in 1791), *The Road to Ruin* (nine editions in 1792), *The Deserted Daughter* (four editions in 1795), and *He's Much to Blame* (four editions in 1798). But he is certainly best known for his novels—*Alwyn* (1780), *Anna St. Ives* (1792), *Hugh Trevor* (1794–1797), *Memoirs of Bryan Perdue* (1805)—and this is also the segment of his corpus the most extensively investigated by scholars.[13] Holcroft's novels show how he progressed from being an advocate of free thought to an architect of revolutionary society. The preface to *Bryan Perdue* reflects his stance: "Whenever I have undertaken to write a novel, I have proposed to myself a specific moral purpose."[14] The topical interest aroused by Holcroft's novels prompted their almost immediate translation on the Continent. In 1792, a German translation of *Anna St. Ives* was published in Berlin by Karl Philipp Moritz (1756–1793) and a French edition appeared in Paris in 1798. The appeal of these novels to foreign readers indicates the occurrence of ideological cross-pollination as well as the reciprocal flow of revolutionary ideology from a beleaguered outpost of reform in Britain to France and Germany, where sympathy for radical alterations to the social fabric, combined with the growing fervor of nationalism, was undiminished. At home in England, however, the situation could not have formed a sharper contrast with the Continent. Following the trial, though exonerated but still considered by many as an enemy

---

13   While Baine (1965), Kelly (1976), and Wallace (2014)—see note 2 above—make giant strides in clarifying the relationship between art and politics in Holcroft's novels, no recent scholarship explores the connection examined in this chapter.

14   Thomas Holcroft, *Memoirs of Bryan Perdue; a Novel* (London: Longman, Hunt, Rees, and Orme, 1805), Vol. I, iii.

of the state, Holcroft's published work could only appear under pseudonyms. As a result, his position as a writer, his sense of identity, and his economic security could not have been more tenuous. In the *Reflections on the Revolution in France* (1790) Burke describes the crucial interdependence between a nation's culture and the state on the one hand, and the maintenance of a theological framework that gives the state its power and *raison d'être*, on the other:

> Nothing is more certain, than that our manners, our civilization, and all good things which are connected with manners and with civilization, have, in this European world of ours, depended for ages on two principles; and were indeed the result of both combined; I mean the spirit of a gentlemen, and the spirit of religion.[15]

In this passage Burke seems to anticipate the position adumbrated by Matthew Arnold in *Culture and Anarchy* (1869) on the relationship between the maintenance of social order and the hegemony of state-sponsored culture:

> [A] State in which law is authoritative and sovereign . . . is requisite if man is to bring to maturity anything precious and lasting . . . . The very framework and exterior order of the State . . . sacred; and culture is the most resolute enemy of anarchy, because of the great hopes and designs for the State which culture teaches us to nourish.[16]

The implications for Holcroft's career are fairly clear: in writing plays and novels that violate generic norms and audience expectations and objectify a critical stance vis-à-vis state authority, he rejects the categorical imperative as stated by Edward Said: "to be for and in culture is to be in and for a State in a compellingly loyal way."[17] The result of such flagrant subversion of the state's aesthetic agenda is cultural disenfranchisement, figurative homelessness,

15   *Selected Writings of Edmund Burke,* ed. Walter Jackson Bate (New York: Modern Library, 1947), 390.
16   Matthew Arnold, *Culture and Anarchy,* ed. J. Dover Wilson (Cambridge: Cambridge University Pres, 1960), 204.
17   Edward Said, *The World, the Text, and the Critic* (Cambridge: Harvard University Press, 1983), 11.

marginalization in the canon, and, ultimately, the silencing of the authorial voice, which amounts to a kind of death. Ventriloquism, or displacing one's voice in translation, becomes the renegade writer's last resort to avoid the complete extinction of literary identity.

Holcroft's slightly abridged translation of Johann Kaspar Lavater's *Physiognomische Fragmente, Essays on the Physiognomy designed to promote the knowledge and love of mankind,* appeared in the same year as Scotsman Henry Hunter's complete edition which was based on Marie-Elisabeth de LaFite's complete French translation, *Essai sur la Physiognomie* (Paris: La Haye, 1781–1803). That Hunter's was the "official" translation is clear; after traveling to Switzerland and obtaining the author's imprimatur, he even engaged Fuseli as a supervisory editor with authority over both the translation of the text and the selection and production of plates, which were produced by the artist Thomas Holloway (1748–1827), best known for his engraved copies of Raphael's cartoons at Windsor Castle. Fuseli also penned the "Advertisement" for the book which contains a vivid biographical sketch of Lavater, a friend in his youth. In contrast to Holcroft's edition, which was published cheaply for the mass market, the edition by Hunter was published by subscription and it appeared in three expensive volumes (1789, 1792, 1798) priced at £30 each.[18] The list of subscribers included other leading intermediaries of German culture, including Taylor, the translator of Goethe's *Iphigenie* (1793), and M.G. "Monk" Lewis, the Gothic novelist, who played a key role in the domestication of the German *Schauerroman* in Britain.[19]

---

18   £90 in 1790 would be worth approximately the equivalent of £10,000 in 2021 (see Measuringworth.com).

19   As a boy of seventeen Lewis met Goethe, "the celebrated author of *Werter* [sic]" in Weimar in 1792. Reporting this event to his mother, he warned her that "you must not be surprised if I shoot myself one of these mornings." Letter dated July 30, 1792 in *The Life and Correspondence of M. G. Lewis,* ed. Margaret Baron-Wilson (London: Henry Colburn Publisher, 1839), quoted in Violet Stockley,

On the strength of its splendid engravings and fine binding, one reviewer considered the lavish Hunter edition "the finest printed book which has ever appeared in this or any other country."[20] Intensifying the rivalry between the two Lavater editions, Holcroft's translation was based on an authorized German abridgement (published by Winterthur, 1783–87) made by Lavater's secretary, J. M. Armbruster (1761–1814). The latter's alterations to the original were approved by Lavater himself in a letter dated 7 April 1783.[21] Complicating matters even further, Holcroft's edition received more favorable attention from the critics than Hunter's. Especially praiseworthy were the notices in *The European Magazine* (XVII and XVIII) and *The Critical Review* (LXVIII and LXIX). The reviewer for the latter incorrectly identified Holcroft's as the first complete version of Lavater's work to appear in English. Such an imperfect reception as that accorded to Hunter's edition could only have provided an additional irritant to Fuseli. This attitude is reflected in his two-part review of Holcroft's translation in the December 1789 and April 1790 issues of the *Analytical*. Fuseli quite correctly indicates that the Holcroft translation was a full volume shorter than Hunter's and he offers a list of Holcroft's translation errors and maladroit passages.

Fuseli's hostile critique was certainly motivated in part by his support for Hunter's translation, but another likely cause of his disapproval was his proprietary interest in the original *Physiognomische Fragmente*. Along with Goethe and others, Fuseli had contributed a number of aphorisms and sketches of heads that were included in the first German language edition (1775). The success of Holcroft's translation also inspired avaricious copycats, including one Samuel Shaw, whose pirated single volume edition

---

German Literature as Known in England 1750–1830 (Port Washington, New York: Kennikat Press, 1969 [1929]), 295.

20   The Monthly Magazine (IX, 1800), quoted in Stockley, *German Literature as Known in England 1750–1830*, 27.

21   Stockley, *German Literature as Known in England 1750–1830*, 28.

appeared in 1792, and an anonymous publisher of the first American edition which was published a year later. Despite any lingering bad blood between Fuseli and Holcroft, the reviewer for the *Analytical* — presumably Fuseli but possibly Wollstonecraft — excoriated the thieving Shaw as "one of those contemptible catchpennies, which cannot be too severely reprehended."[22] In 1792 G.G.J. and J. Robinson, Holcroft's publisher, responded to the threat of further piracy by issuing a one-volume abridgement that featured none of the inaccuracies that marred Shaw's hastily executed literary theft. Hunter's expensively printed translation from the French was in turn pirated by another clergyman, the Rev. C. Moore, whose edition was published in 1797. Despite its limitations, in both legal and pirated editions, Holcroft's translation remained the standard English version of Lavater's *Fragmente* throughout the nineteenth and early twentieth centuries.

Not all of Holcroft's translations created internecine rivalry within the Godwin Circle as his Lavater edition did. As a rule, his work as a translator reflected a knack for choosing texts with undeniable commercial appeal. Not untypical was the success enjoyed by his adaptation of *The Marriage of Figaro*, entitled *Follies of the Day*, which was performed on December 4, 1784 at Covent Garden with Holcroft in the lead role. Other French authors he translated included Stéphanie Félicité du Crest de Saint-Aubin (1746–1830), Claude-Étienne Savary (1750–1788), and Marie Jules César Sauvigny (1777–1851). Another successful play, Holcroft's 1790 translation of J. C. Brandes's *The German Hotel*, was frequently performed and reprinted throughout the decade. Holcroft also enjoyed success with the first English translations of Stolberg's *Travels through Germany, Switzerland, Italy, and Sicily* (1796)[23] — Fuseli's review appeared in

---

22   *Johann Caspar Lavater Correspondence* (Electronic Enlightenment Project, 2008), Vol. XIII, 427.

23   The career of Stolberg (1750–1819), who was a friend of Goethe, formed a bridge between the *Sturm und Drang* of the 1770s and *fin-de-siécle* German Romanticism. He was a translator of Homer (1778), Plato (1796/97), Ossian (1806), and a

the December 1797 *Analytical Review* (XXVI)—and the *Life of Baron Frederic Trenck* (London, 1788; Boston, 1792),[24] which has been continuously in print ever since. At this time the demand for works of real adventures was such that two other translations of Trenck's novelistic, exotic memoirs were published—anonymously—in the same year.

Holcroft's selection of these texts to translate exemplifies the special nature of his relationship with German literature. Both works afforded opportunities for submerged self-expression in the colorful careers of two liberal members of the German aristocracy which he donned in place of his own identity as an exiled, impoverished Jacobin author, subject to censorship, who was *persona non grata* in Britain following the treason trial. Stolberg's and Trenck's memoirs—as encounters with foreign otherness—reflect the substitution of Holcroft's voice in place of other "voices"; they also served as paradigms for his original *Travels from Hamburg, through Westphalia, Holland, and the Netherlands, to Paris* (1804). Holcroft's own encounter with Northern Europe must therefore be mediated by his translations of others' travel writing—and possibly also by his reading of Wollstonecraft's *A Short Residence in Sweden, Norway, and Denmark* (1796). Holcroft's editions of Stolberg and Trenck indicate that for him translation functioned as a displacement of original writing—an extreme sign of self-censorship—and represented an appropriation of an "alternative" culture in place of the official state-sponsored literary culture in Britain from which Jacobins, dissenters, women and others were excluded and marginalized.

---

prominent member of the "Göttinger Dichterkreis" led by Ludwig Christian Heinrich Hölty (1748–1776).

24   Trenck's Life, translated by Holcroft, which is subtitled "HIS ADVENTURES and CRUEL and EXCESSIVE SUFFERINGS DURING AN IMPRISONMENT OF TEN YEARS in the fortress of Magdeburg, by command of the late King of Prussia," surely inspired Godwin's bleak portrayal of Reginald de St. Leon's confinement in Bethlem Gabor's castle in *St. Leon* (1799), Vol. III. Holcroft's translation has been reprinted in multiple editions as recently as 2016 (see Amazon.com).

Referring to "the occasional dilemmas of the Translator," Holcroft's Preface to Stolberg's *Travels* gives some indication of his authorial insecurity. The following passage is highly self-referential in disclosing the difficulties faced in mediating the *terra incognita* of Stolberg's experiences: in "following his erratic and devious path . . . the Translator has not infrequently found himself in a labyrinth, from which to extricate himself, and never lose sight of his author, was a task of difficulty and address." As for his confrontation with the original German he speaks of its "complex construction, indefinite grammar, licentious orthography, and perplexed idiom."[25]

The most important of Holcroft's translations in literary-historical terms—and his greatest challenge of this kind—is of Goethe's narrative poem, *Hermann und Dorothea* (1801), which was the first to appear in Britain. With this translation Holcroft joined a select company of Goethe's British intermediaries, including Taylor, Walter Scott, Crabb Robinson, Sarah Austin, and Carlyle. As an alternative to disclosing the otherness of the existing order in Britain and the alienation that he and his fellow Jacobins and dissenters experienced on the margins of their native culture—the positing of such otherness which had characterized his activity as a novelist, playwright, and journalist before his arrest—the translation of Goethe's text served as an exercise in centering himself in a foreign otherness. This otherness is nonetheless not entirely unfamiliar to him, since the conflict facing Hermann's family in the poem is similar to the cultural dilemma confronting Holcroft and other British radicals in the wake of war hysteria and government reaction: how does one adjust to the chaos and alienation of war thrust upon their settled existence by French invaders? And yet the means appear for restoring the shattered idyll and reconciling Hermann and his parents to life, and this means comes to them in the form of Dorothea the refugee. She offers a critique of the way things are while yet offering a good deal of idealistic rhetoric about the possibility of

---

25   Stolberg, *Travels*, vi, vii.

repairing the damaged fabric of society which will lead to the rec-
onciliation of the alienated individual with society and the state. In
fact, Goethe's poem extols many of the values associated with religious and political Dissent. But because of his status as an outsider
in British culture even before his arrest, Holcroft was never in his
own novels or plays able to attain the state of unified perception
between subject and object—the self and the social world—visible
in his translation. This condition, which is analogous to Bakhtinian
"transgredience," is produced when "the whole existence of others
is seen from outside not only their own knowledge that they are
being perceived by somebody else, but from beyond their awareness that such an other even exists."[26] Holcroft thus approached the
task of translating *Hermann und Dorothea* as an attempt to attain
"transgredience" between the author of the original work and himself as the mediator of its otherness.

Goethe himself noticed this quality in Holcroft's translation.
In a letter to Holcroft dated May 29, 1801 Goethe distinguishes between two approaches to translation: the first, in which the translator tries "seiner Nation den reinen Begriff eines fremden Autors
überliefern, fremde Zustände derselben anschaulich machen will,
wobei man sich denn genau an das Original bindet" [to convey the
pure concept of a foreign author, to make the foreign context vividly realizable to the reader, by binding himself precisely to the
original meaning].[27] Alternatively, the translator may choose to

26   Michael Holquist, *Dialogism: Bakhtin and his World* (London: Routledge, 1990),
     33.

27   Johann Wolfgang von *Goethe, Briefe der Jahre 1786–1814 in Gedenkausgabe der
     Werke, Briefe und Gespräche. Band 19*, ed. Ernst Beutler (Zürich: Artemis Verlag,
     1949), Vol. XIX, 409–410: „Indem ich die mir mitgeteilte Übersetzung von Her-
     mann und Dorothea mit Dank zurücksende erlauben Sie mir, wertgeschätzer
     Herr, einige Betrachtungen. Man kann wie es mir scheint, nach zweierlei Maxi-
     men übersetzen, einmal wenn man seiner Nation den reinen Begriff eines frem-
     den Autors überliefern, fremde Zustände derselben anschaulich machen will,
     wobei man sich denn genau an das Original bindet; man kann aber auch ein
     solches fremdes Werk als eine Art Stoff behandeln, indem man es, nach eignen
     Empfindungen und Überzeugungen, dergestalt verändert, daß es unserer

treat the original text as "eine Art Stoff," that is, a pliable medium which may be modified in such a way "that it becomes more familiar" to the translator's readers, even to the point where "his readers will be able to read it as an original," as though the text's otherness had been neutralized. The latter technique, Goethe insists, is Holcroft's method, which is in keeping with the description Holcroft provides concerning his methodology in the Preface and Notes to the translation:

> In moral sentiments, poetical feeling, and idioms of speech, Each people have their peculiarities. To these I have not infrequently dared to render my author subject; and indulge in such variations as I imagined he would have been likely to have adopted, had he written to the English Nation . . . . [The translator] will not honour his author by being too much his slave; though continual attempts to be his equal are but continual disappointments: at least, such honours are rarely attained, and short of duration; and even while he seeks them, he exposes himself to the dangers either of just censure or pedantic cavil.[28]

Nation näher gebracht und von ihr gleichsam als ein Originalwerk aufgenommen werden könne. In dem letzten Falle scheinen Sie sich zu befinden. Sie haben zwar im ganzen den Gang meines Gedichtes beibehalten, aber durchaus, soviel ich beurteilen kann, die dramatisch charakteristischen, läßlichen Äußerungen meiner Personen strenger, auffanllender, didaktischer überliefert, und die gemächliche epische Bewegung in einen ernsteren gemeßnern Schritt verwandelt. Nach meiner wenigen Einsicht in die englische Literatur darf ich schließen daß Sie hierbei den Charakter Ihrer Nation vor Augen gehabt, und es ist mir um so angenehmer eine völlige Aufklärung hierüber in der Vorrede und den Noten, welche Sie Ihrer Arbeit beizufügen gedenken, nächstens zu erhalten. Übrigens kann ich die meisten Abweichungen vom Original aus meinem gefaßten Standpunkte ziemlich beurteilen, nur vermag ich nicht einzusehen warum Sie die Stelle, vom hundertsechsundzwanzigsten Vers Ihrer Übersetzungen an, bis zum hundertzweiundvierzigsten, auf den ehemaligen Brand des Städtchens gedeutet, da, im Original, dieser längst vergangenen Begebenheit nur im Vorbeigehen erwähnt und eigentlich die Beschreibung des Zuges der Ausgewanderten durch diese Stelle fortgesetzt wird. Doch erhalte ich wohl auch hierüber einige Belehrung und ergreife vielleicht irgend eine Gelegenheit über die vier, nunmehr von mir liegenden, Übersetzungen meines Gedichtes öffentlich meine Gedanken zu sagen. Der ich recht wohl zu leben wünsche und mich zu geneigtem Andenken empfehle."

28   Johann Wolfgang von Goethe, *Hermann and Dorothea*, trans. Thomas Holcroft (London: T. N. Longman and O. Rees, 1801), xii, 181.

Holcroft's commentary on Goethe's poem also contains an implicit theory of translation which suggests parallels with essayist William Hazlitt's concept of "gusto" or Keatsean "intensity." Clearly, for Holcroft, the focus of the translator is on replicating emotional authenticity rather than word-for-word accuracy:

> A poet can never be translated with any due degree of the enthusiasm with which he wrote, unless the translator excites in himself the same kind of ardor. He will then, while he breathes spirit and feeling of his author, generally forget his author's words. The excellence of all translations will indeed rather consist in the feeling and the spirit than in the words.[29]

The process of selection and arrangement of suitable voices and garb for the transformation of the foreign text into something new and yet non-alienating is itself perhaps a more adequate definition for the search for a specific framework from a multitude of possible responses. And here, in Goethe's translated text, at a significant site of cultural interaction in the Romantic Age, Holcroft appears to have attained reciprocal unity between subject and object to a degree that eluded him in his career as novelist, playwright, and journalist.

William Taylor of Norwich

Writing for the comparatively liberal and cosmopolitan *Monthly Review*, William Taylor emerged as a key figure in the cultural politics of the 1790s. Less familiar to us, perhaps, than the translators Robert Pearse Gillies (1788–1858) and John Gibson Lockhart (1794–1854), the son-in-law of Sir Walter Scott, Taylor is nonetheless the most important critic of German literature before Carlyle who stimulated

---

29 *Hermann und Dorothea*, trans. Holcroft, 180. Holcroft makes the same point in his Preface to Stolberg's *Travels*: "Imagination . . . holds a looser rein; her track is aerial; and, though dazzling, closes instantly upon the view. To trace her capricious course in an exact line is impossible; and those who translate poetry must not pore over the words of the author, but imbibe his feelings, animate themselves with the same fires, and soar on the same daring wing" (ix).

the German studies of Crabb Robinson, Scott, Lewis, George Barrow, Sarah Austin, and the future poet laureate Robert Southey. His career as a translator and critic encapsulates the problems confronting would-be British mediators of foreign culture at the close of the eighteenth century. There is, as in Coleridge, a certain logical consistency running through Taylor's opinions, but also insensitivity to the special development in literary history represented by Goethe. Wilhelm Dilthey (1833–1911), for one, suggested that the difficulties Goethe's contemporaries experienced in classifying him result from the confusing array of talents and interests that he embodied. The likelihood of misinterpretation is also increased by Goethe's ambivalent relationship to the *Aufklärung* [Enlightenment]. Although Goethe shares a common cultural legacy with Klopstock, for example, to whom Coleridge and Wordsworth paid a visit in 1798, his characteristic form of literary expression is lyrical, generically unstable, and highly subjective. Many British critics of the time, including Taylor, Coleridge, Hazlitt, and De Quincey, did not recognize that Goethe's manner of expressing himself represented a radical new departure in modern thought and literature. In addition to his literary work, Goethe's scientific research, philosophical reflections, and even his administrative duties for the Grand Duchy of Saxe-Weimar, form a seamless unity with and do not simply fill in the pauses separating his creative periods.

If the important new functions of the poet fused in Goethe went unnoticed by many influential contemporaries—consider Adolf Menzel (1857–1838) in Germany and Taylor, Coleridge, Hazlitt, and De Quincey in Britain—more conventional writers posed no such problems. For example, the works of August von Kotzebue (1761–1819), Taylor's literary idol, enjoyed enormous popularity on the London stage. "According to my judgment," Taylor writes in tones of praise so immoderate that he elicited Carlyle's "good-humored" and "judicial censure"[30] in the *Edinburgh Review*: "Kotzebue

---

30   Saintsbury, Vol. III, 497.

is the greatest dramatic genius that Europe has evolved since Shakespeare." Taylor was determined "to give some idea of the various powers of this great writer," whose range includes "plays of every form: farces, melodramas, mixt or sentimental dramas, household tragedies, classical tragedies, and . . . that vaster and more difficult form of art . . . the gothic tragedy."[31] Kotzebue's apparent defects, including his notorious prolificity and nonchalance, are, in Taylor's estimation, signs of genius. He applauds Kotzebue's penchant for grandiose special effects even at the expense of nuances of character, plot development, and dialogue. These "extraordinary" effects "concentrate the attention of an audience on the passing scene."[32] Even though Taylor concedes that "Goethe had the merit of showing" others "the way" and of having surpassed both Kotzebue and Schiller in classical tragedy with *Iphigenia in Tauris*, he nonetheless praises Kotzebue for his "superior invention," in which he excels Schiller and Goethe. Moreover, his "comic approaches his tragic force . . . and his sudden power over all the emotions has in it something magical."[33] Accustomed to Kotzebue's energy, pathos, and sentimentality, Taylor was not aesthetically inclined to admire the realism of Goethe's diction, his naturalistic portrayal of human passions, and his indifference to neoclassical conventions of pacing or time.

Taylor was baffled by the changes in Goethe's artistic development that took place in the fifty years dividing *Werther* from *Wilhelm Meister*. The abstractions of Goethe's later style and the focus on the protagonist's inner development as he experiences a broad panorama of human experience created puzzles for a critic with a predilection for sentiment, decorum, and sensationalistic stage effects. Although he approves of the "picturesque descriptions, sage reflections, and poignant situations" that are found in the novel,

31   William Taylor, *An Historic Survey of German Poetry*, 3 Volumes (London: Treutel and Würtz, 1828–1830), Vol. II, 102.
32   Taylor, Vol. III, 102–103.
33   Taylor, Vol. III, 376–377.

Taylor notes that "a senile garrulity creeps on him, his style is become more trailing, and those gushes of learning, which refresh the soul, sparkle seldomer along the smoother but expanded currents of his narrative."[34]

Taylor's survey of Goethe's major works in prose continues in the same vein of moral reproach and aesthetic disapproval. He dismisses *Die Wahlverwandschaften* [*Elective Affinities*] (1809) as "hardly worthy" of Goethe's pen. Although he is prepared to acknowledge Goethe's superior "knowledge of human nature," ingeniously represented as analogous to certain kinds of chemical reaction, he sees in this performance "some declension of his plastic power."[35] Taylor's remarks on *Dichtung und Wahrheit* suggests that he fails to recognize the organization and method of the work and its relation to Goethe's Terentian openness to human experience:

> This is not an autobiography, but rather a biographical novel, in which many things are related of the hero, which never happened to him. It is a household epopeia, which, like the Waverly novels [of Walter Scott], mingles history and invention, in a manner interesting to the reader, but dangerous to his distinctness of memory, particularly as, in this instance, he cannot turn to the pure chronicle of the historian.[36]

In translating *Dichtung und Wahrheit* with the terms reversed, as "Fact and Fiction," Taylor misconstrued the significance of the juxtaposition of "Dichtung" and "Wahrheit." In Goethe's title the emphasis is on "Dichtung." Subordinate to "Dichtung" in Goethe's title is "Wahrheit," which is not adequately translated as "fact," but should actually be characterized as "truth." Taylor's description of *Dichtung und Wahrheit* as a kind of domestic epic is in fact an astute observation. As a "biographical novel" *Dichtung und Wahrheit* reveals what Arthur Schopenhauer describes as the "innere Bedeutsamkeit" [inner significance] of everyday life in contrast to the

---

34   Taylor, Vol. III, 362.
35   Taylor, Vol. III, 349.
36   Taylor, Vol. III, 376.

"äussere Bedeutsamkeit" [outer significance] of historical narrative.[37] And yet, because Taylor blames Goethe for failing "to separate the fiction from the fact" in this work, it is clear that he has
profoundly misunderstood Goethe's technique of interpreting his
age through the medium of his own personality and the formative
events in his development.[38] His perplexity anticipates late nineteenth-century critic George Saintsbury's denunciation of techniques of criticism in which the main emphasis is on the personality of the author. Goethe gives the scenes "from my life" a "typical" quality that corresponds to Aristotle's concept of "universal-
ity," Sir Philip Sidney's Horatian "speaking picture of Poesy," Hegel's "concrete universal," and T.S. Eliot's "objective correlative."
As the leading poet of his age and *Sprachraum*,[39] Goethe creates
out of the raw materials of his life an artistic mythos, in which the
constituent elements—poetry and truth, the universal idea and
the particular event—are kept in balance. Taylor denigrates the
book's mythical dimension as merely "a spirit of omen-hunting,
hardly consistent with the complete infidelity, to which Goethe
lays claim."[40]

Taylor's judgment of Goethe did not evolve. Even Crabb Robinson's friendly disagreement and Carlyle's negative review left
him unrepentant, but it is important to note that even the favorable
views of Crabb Robinson and Carlyle signified rare outbursts of
dissent in an age dominated by nearly universal antipathy toward
Goethe. The congruence between Taylor's views and the editorial
position of *The Anti-Jacobin Review* is apparent in a letter sent to
Crabb Robinson in the summer of 1813 on the taste of the British
reading public and the reception of Goethe's immorality:

---

37   Arthur Schopenhauer, *Die Welt als Wille und Vorstellung*, ed. Werner Brede (Mu-
nich: Carl Hauser Verlag, 1977), Bk. 3, Par. 48, 304.
38   Taylor, *An Historic Survey of German Poetry*, Vol. III, 376.
39   This is a more accurate designation than "nation," which, in the modern sense,
does not come into existence until nearly forty years after Goethe's death.
40   Taylor, *An Historic Survey of German Poetry*, Vol. III, 376.

> The entire works of Goethe would not suit here: he has attained that divine morality which looks down on all forms of human conduct, which equal eye, and sees in the lewdness of Faustus, or the purity of Iphigenie, but that exact adaptation of effect and cause, of conduct and motive, which he characterizes the constitution of things.[41]

Shortly afterward, Crabb Robinson recorded a conversation with Taylor that took place on August 19, 1813: "In the evening a call on W. Taylor late. We talked on German literature in which Taylor is a heretic, for he does not acknowledge the supremacy of Goethe."[42]

Taylor's limitations as a critic and cultural mediator are perhaps nowhere more apparent than in his misjudgment of Goethe. For example, while Goethe shares a common cultural legacy with Lessing, his poetic gift and his sensibility, which encode highly personal feelings and experiences, are at odds with Enlightenment ideals of detachment and objectivity. Taylor was not alone in failing to recognize that Goethe's subjectivity represented a radical new departure; one recalls that while traveling in Germany Coleridge and Wordsworth anachronistically beat a path to Klopstock's door. Coleridge also planned to write a full-scale study of Lessing's life and works. In step with Coleridge, whose response to Schiller's Karl Moor is well known ("Southey, who is this convulser of the heart?"), Taylor esteems Kotzebue's energy and Schiller's sublimity over Goethe's naturalism.

Despite his shortcomings as a mediator and translator of German culture in Britain—flaws that he shared with much more eminent contemporaries, Taylor may be singled out as arguably the most important early initiator of intercultural and interlinguistic exchange between Britain and Germany. The difficulties he faced—from a proliferation of faulty translations to censorship—simply indicate, as the translation theorist Antoine Berman has argued, that "every culture resists translation"—and the fact that the current crisis over European unity issues from Britain is additional evidence

---

41   Cited Norman, Vol. I, 64.
42   Cited in Norman, Vol. I, 70.

of such resistance. Even Taylor's modest accomplishments as a reviewer and translator reinforce Berman's view that "the very aim of translation [is] to open up in writing a certain relation with the Other, to fertilize what is one's Own through the mediation of what is Foreign." Translation is thus "diametrically opposed to the ethnocentric structure of every culture, that species of narcissism by which every society wants to be a pure and unadulterated Whole . . . . The essence of translation may be likened to an opening, a dialogue, a cross-breeding, a de-centering" of one's culture that inevitably provides resistance of the sort represented by the *Anti-Jacobin* and *The Anti-Jacobin Review*.[43] Politically motivated resistance to the importation of foreign texts in Britain is to blame for the deformations in Taylor's response to German literature, such as his anachronistic preference for Kotzebue over Goethe (as it does for Coleridge and Wordsworth's initial preference for Klopstock).

Imperfect as they may be, the translations by Holcroft and Taylor fulfill the essential function of incarnating cross-border cultural exchanges. Regardless of their quality their translations arise from a multiplicity of intercultural and interlinguistic acts. As the French critic Berman has suggested, these are "interactions in which they construct their own identity and their relations to the foreign." Thus, translation is the essence of the formation of the self—and by extension, an entire people—which demands the appropriation of otherness in a form that makes contact possible and fulfilling. The movement of translation like that of *Bildung* is circular and "starts from what is one's own, the same, in order to go towards the foreign, the other . . . and, starting from this experience, to return to its point of departure."[44] Since unmediated experience of the other is not possible, appropriation of the foreign takes the form of an annexation, a use of difference, the foreign, and the past, for the needs of the self, the familiar, and the present.

---

43   Antoine Berman, *The Experience of the Foreign: Culture and Translation in Romantic Germany* (Albany, New York: State University of New York Press, 1992), 4.

44   *Ibid.*, 46.

8 Generic Fusion in the Romantic Travel Novel

> "There are no books which I more delight in than Travels, especially those that describe remote countries, and give the Writer an Opportunity of showing his Parts without any Danger of being examined or contradicted."
>
> Richard Steele, *Tatler No. 254* (1710)

> "The décor is verifiable, one must not lie . . . . By the exactitude of the décor the novelist makes credible the human verity of his characters, he makes a success of his lies."
>
> Louis Aragon, *L'Abats mon jeu* (1959)

> ". . . that crucial moment in modern thought when, thanks to the great voyages of discovery, a human community which had believed itself to be complete, and in its final form suddenly learned . . . that it was not alone, that it was part of a greater whole, and that, in order to achieve self-knowledge, it must first of all contemplate its unrecognizable image in this mirror."
>
> Claude Lévi-Strauss, *Tristes Tropiques* (1955)

To literary historians William Godwin may be best remembered for having been related to writers of more enduring achievement than his own. Indicating that little has changed in nearly 200 years, Thomas De Quincey's epitaph for Godwin corresponds in large part to our century's judgment: "he is remembered less by the novels that succeeded, or by the philosophy that he abjured than as the man that had Mary Wollstonecraft for his wife, Mrs. Shelley for his daughter, and the immortal Shelley as his son-in-law."[1] This assessment has long obscured Godwin's achievement as a novelist. Although the British government's crackdown on the reform movement (with which he was closely associated) during the 1790s did

---

1   Thomas DeQuincey, *DeQuincey's Collected Works*, Vol. XI, 335.

result in a permanent decline in his influence and popularity, Godwin continued to produce large-scale novels at regular intervals until his death in 1836—*Caleb Williams* (1794), *St. Leon* (1799), *Fleetwood* (18050, *Mandeville* (1817), *Cloudesley* (1830), and *Deloraine* (1833). *Caleb Williams*, the only canonical novel in the group, is prized by critics as a pioneering venture in detective fiction, but in every subsequent novel Godwin eschews repetition of previous formulas, however successful.

St. Leon: A Tale of the 16th Century, Godwin's most innovative novel, incorporates within a framework of modified but recognizable conventions of travel literature elements of the historical and Gothic novels, the Romance, and *Bildungsroman*. To a degree unmatched by other English novels of the Romantic Period, *St. Leon* exemplifies the function of "romantische poesie" as defined by Friedrich Schlegel (1772–1829) in the "Athenäums-Fragment No. 116" (1798):

> Romantic poetry is a progressive universal poetry. It is destined not merely to reunite the separate genres of poetry and to link poetry to philosophy and rhetoric . . . . Romantic poetry alone can, like the epic, become a mirror to the whole surrounding world, an image of its age. At the same time, free of all real and ideal interests, it can also float on wings of poetic reflection midway between the work and the artist, constantly reinforcing this reflection and multiplying it as in an unending series of mirrors.

The novel's generic combinations and fusions are reflected in the repeated metamorphoses of Godwin's sorcerer protagonist, whose travels across the European continent confront the central Romantic problem of mediating and appropriating the foreign. The novel also serves as a vehicle for Godwin's ideological concerns and the observant reader notices analogies, for instance, between the controversy surrounding the protagonist's use of the philosopher's stone and the Revolution Controversy (1789–1795) in England. More generally, the novel presents an interpretation of a transitional moment in sixteenth-century intellectual history, which involved the epistemological shift from alchemy to modern chemistry and, in politics and the social sphere, from chivalry and feudalism to the inchoate institutions of capitalism. To read *St. Leon* requires the reconstruction of intellectual and literary history and the mediation of geographical, historical, and political symbolism. In the reading of the novel that follows observations are offered on the sources and antecedents, in prose fiction and travel writing, for the different elements contributing to the generic diversity exhibited in the novel.

After a long prelude covering the protagonist's education, which includes a harrowing brush with death at the Battle of Pavia (February 24, 1525)—a powerful set piece that demonstrates Godwin's epic range and command of historical details—the reader encounters Reginald de St. Leon, the flower of sixteenth-century French chivalry. But after he squanders his family fortune on the gaming tables of Paris his fall from grace is swift. Forced by the stigma of dishonor to retreat from society Reginald settles his wife and children on the banks of Lake Constance in northern Switzerland. In this pastoral episode Godwin presents an inversion of the Rousseauian utopia, which is achieved not prior to the formation but after the dissolution of social bonds between individuals. There is, in Marguerite de St. Leon's response to their arrival in pre-Napoleonic Switzerland, echoes of Godwin's "New Philosophy," including a post-*Lyrical Ballads* idealization of the peasantry as the basis of a free, classless society:

> it is, I fear, too true, that the splendour in which we lately lived has its basis in oppression; and that the superfluities of the rich are a boon extorted from the hunger and misery of the poor! Here we see a peasantry more peaceful and less oppressed than perhaps any other tract of the earth can exhibit. They are erect and independent, at once friendly and fearless. Is not this a refreshing spectacle: I now begin practically to perceive that the cultivators of the fields and the vineyards are my brethren and my sisters; and my heart bounds with joy, as I feel my relations to society multiply. How cumbrous is magnificence! The moderate man is the only free! (II: 241)[2]

---

2   All quoted passages from the novel are from the first edition: William Godwin, *St. Leon: A Tale of the Sixteenth Century*, 3 Volumes (London: Printed for G.G. and J. Robinson by R. Noble, printer. 1799).

The peace and harmony of Reginald's idyll is short-lived; the family's isolation is broken by the appearance of Zampieri, a sickly old man with a mysterious air. Before his death he imparts to Reginald the occult powers of alchemy—the philosopher's stone and the *elixir vitae*—which bestow infinite wealth and eternal life on their possessor. But his gift is granted on condition that his secret not be shared with anyone, including Marguerite. A mania for secrecy destroys the bonds of sincere and open communication by which the family's utopia was originally secured. Reacting to rumors that ill-gotten wealth is being hoarded in the family cottage, Swiss authorities arrive and arrest him. Reginald is imprisoned, casting further aspersions on the family's honor. The resulting humiliation compounds the embarrassment of recent events in France and Reginald's son Charles, a true representative of chivalry, feels compelled to leave home, vowing to make his father pay for the blot on the family's honor.

Prison walls are no match for the corrupting powers of gold, and with the philosopher's stone and small quantities of sulfur, salt, and mercury, Reginald is able to bribe his Swiss guards. But following his escape, continued freedom is purchased only by perpetual flight. Hounded by the authorities from one end of Europe to the other, Reginald and Marguerite lead a fugitive existence that has great resonance for the Romantic Period and the combination of tragedy and pathos in their experience bears comparison with other Romantic outcasts, such as Faust, Cain, Childe Harold, Manfred, and Prometheus. Their travels across Europe are also a haunting anticipation of P. B. and Mary Shelley's ill-fated migrations. Their flight and persecution also suggest parallels to the suppression of dissent in the 1790 by the British government's campaign of censorship, trials for treason, and transportation of the convicted.

Taking leave of Switzerland for refuge in Italy, Reginald and family adopt the name Boismorand. But rumors of infernal practices precede them and soon they must flee a predatory mob. Prior to embarking for Spain, Marguerite delivers a stillborn baby. Soon after, in a direct allusion to Mary Wollstonecraft, Marguerite dies of complications of childbirth. Reginald ascribes his multiple losses to "the stranger," but blames himself for the destruction of Marguerite, "the better half of my soul," a stand-in for Mary Wollstonecraft. (III: 129) Fearing for the safety of his daughters, he seems to himself "like the far-famed tree of India [cerbera odollam or Suicide Tree], to be destined to shelter only to destroy, and to prove a deadly poison to whatever sought its refuge under my protecting branches." (III: 134) The young girls are placed in the protective custody of a woman, one Mariana—another Wollstonecraft double—whose most becoming quality as a protectress is her resemblance to their deceased mother. Another change of identity takes place, this time to Valmine, "guardian of the orphan heiresses of St. Leon." Reginald seeks atonement for his sense of guilt for Marguerite's death by vowing to apply his secrets solely for the benefit of mankind. His benevolent gestures are, however, thwarted at every turn and lead, ironically, to intensified persecution by suspicious local authorities throughout Europe.

In yet another scene of brilliant local color which seems an innocuous pastime, St. Leon-Valmine attends a bullfight where he sees a familiar face in the crowd. Previously introduced as the hospitable nobleman whose solicitude dupes the honor- and friendship-starved alchemist into sharing some conversation, this individual turns out to be a spy for the "holy inquisition." St. Leon-Valmine is then arrested and, as he enters the labyrinth of the legal arm of the Church, St. Leon-Valmine comments on the nature of the Church's power. Godwin's reader is free to draw parallels with the British government's reaction to the reform movement and the threat of revolution: "The present was the most important crisis that ever occurred in the history of the world. There was a spirit at work, that aimed at the dissolving all the bonds of civil society, and converting mankind into beasts and savages." (III: 187) And, in a passage that reads like a verbatim passage from *Political Justice*, St. Leon-Valmine concludes that a religion "which is supported by such means" — the naked exercise of power — "is viler than atheism. That civilization which has its buttress in despotism, is more worthless and hateful than the state of savages running wild in their woods." (III: 198) By alluding to Godwin the philosopher, Godwin the novelist demonstrates the operation of a mind that fuses imagination and intellect, creation and analysis. This phenomenon inspired William Hazlitt (1778–1830), in an article entitled "Mr. Godwin" in *The Edinburgh Review* (1830), to describe Godwin's literary achievement as the result of supernatural intervention. To many observers both kinds of writing seem "as distinct as to style and subject matter, as if two different persons wrote them. No one in reading the philosophical treatise would suspect the embryonic romance: those who personally know Mr. Godwin would as little anticipate either . . . . It is as if a magician had produced some mighty feat of his art without warning." But as discordant as these two modes of writing may have seemed to many contemporary readers, Hazlitt considers that "from the philosophical to the romantic visionary there was but one step."[3] This observation corresponds to Schlegel's view of Romanticism, alluded to above, as embodying a syncretic appropriation of all forms of literary discourse that results in a radical cosmopolitanism.

As it happens, St. Leon-Valmine is imprisoned for twelve years before being tried and then condemned for heresy by the Spanish Inquisition. In the historical homeland of alchemy, which was originally imported into Spain by the Moors, the Roman Catholic Church is, perhaps, even more stridently dedicated to stamping out what it perceives as invocation of black magic, infernal powers — that grew up on Spanish soil.[4] Reginald escapes the *auto-da-fé* by taking refuge with a Jewish family headed by an elderly

---

3   William Hazlitt, "Mr. Godwin" (1830), *Contributions to the Edinburgh Review,* in *The Complete Works of William Hazlitt,* ed. P.P. Howe (London: J.M. and Sons, Ltd., 1932), Vol. XV, 403. All intra-textual references are to this edition.

4   For a concise history of alchemy, see *The Encyclopedia of Religion and Ethics,* ed. James Hastings (New York: Charles Scribner's Sons, 1928), Vol. I, 287–298.

patriarch. This outcast people are treated sympathetically in large part because they, like Godwin himself, are non-Christians: "for the first time [in twelve years] I had the opportunity to communicate with a man whose soul was not enslaved to the blood-thirsty superstition of this devoted country." (III: 257) On this occasion, Reginald initiates the use of the *elixir vitae*, which sends him into a deep *Heilschlaf* from which he awakes as a much younger man. Thus disguised, he pays a visit to his daughters, Julia and Louisa, who have grown to maturity. He finds to his dismay Julia and her fiancé have committed suicide; they were denied permission to marry on account of her father's reputation: "Fatal legacy! atrocious secrets of medicine and chemistry! everyday opened to my astonished and terrified sight a wider prospect of their wasteful effects." (IV: 26)

"The outcast of my species," without friends or family, Reginald travels to Hungary, a country situated on the margins of Europe. (IV: 35) Here, in 1560, standing between Christian west and Muslim east, he finds a new identity, a place of refuge, and, apparently, a just cause to serve: "I resolved to pour the entire stream of my riches like a mighty river, to fertilize these wasted plains." (IV:43) Caught in a war between the Holy Roman Empire under the Emperor Charles V and the Turks under Suleiman the Magnificent, the people of Hungary are suffering the pangs of famine. Reginald, whose ability to manufacture wealth pays for huge shipments of grain, becomes intoxicated with the power to preserve life and to foster gratitude and acceptance: "[S]hould I not have a right, to expect to find myself guarded by the faithful love of a people, who would be indebted to my beneficence for every breath they drew?" (IV: 43) Like Goethe's (1774),[5] Beethoven's (1801), and Byron's

---

5   The first English translation of Goethe's "Prometheus" was published by Henry Crabb Robinson in 1802–03. The final stanza emphasizes Prometheus's humanity and unslaked defiance of Zeus: "Here I sit and form/A man like myself;/A race like me,/To suffer and to weep;/And have enjoyment,/And to despise,/As I do thee."

(1816) Prometheus, as well as Mary's Victor Frankenstein, Reginald seeks to "be a father to the human race," to find a community to which he can belong, but he does not count on the ingratitude of his adopted "children." (IV: 185)

Reginald's altruism stirs the jealousy of the sultan and the ingratitude of the very people whom he sought to help. This reaction is not undeserved, as he himself observes somewhat earlier, since an enormous supply of imported foodstuffs inevitably undermines the free market for all commodities and a mysterious infusion of gold debases the monetary system, leading to the ruin of other essential social institutions: "Exhaustless wealth, if communicated to all men, would be but an exhaustless heap of pebbles and dust; and nature will not admit the everlasting laws to be so abrogated, as they would be by rendering the whole race of sublunary man immortal." (II: 103) Facing the wrath of the mob, on the one hand, and the wrath of the Ottoman Empire on the other, he is forced once again to take flight. Reginald seeks refuge with Bethlem Gabor, a sublime misanthropic figure, who had once been his loyal friend and fellow pariah, but whose cupidity has obviously overwhelmed his love.

Gabor's character is not the only Gothic convention encountered in the protagonist's travels. And while Godwin employs much of the stock-in-trade of the Gothic, including medieval castles, sublime landscapes, a gallery of mysterious figures, various inexplicable happenings, and, of course, the brooding presence of the supernatural, he explores other applications of the Romance tradition besides the subversion of the Romance and its modern analogue, the Gothic, in versions of the anti-Romance and the Gothic-manqué. Typical of Godwin's method of exploiting readers' expectations by simultaneously encouraging and frustrating them, is the use of his romance device laden novel for didactic purposes. While many voices were raised in the seventeenth and eighteenth centuries condemning novels as frivolous or even dangerous—such as that of Nicolas Boileau (1636–1711), Pierre Defontaines (1685–1745),

Anthony Ashley Cooper, 3rd Earl of Shaftesbury (1671–1713), Daniel Defoe (1660–1731), Samuel Richardson (1689–1761), Samuel Johnson in *Rambler No. 4* (31 March 1750), and Jane Austen (1775–1817)—Godwin allows serious moral and psychological analysis to piggyback the fantastic travels of his constantly metamorphosing protagonist. However, in yet one more unexpected departure from generic consistency, Godwin frames the supernatural and the fantastic in *St. Leon* with remarkable historical accuracy and concrete visualization of places and events as well as sixteenth-century manners and morals.

Despite the presence of the above-mentioned Gothic devices, the novel's central concerns are, first, the realistic presentation of the protagonist's guilt-ridden psyche and, secondly, a pre-Nietzschean analysis of the will to power. This shifting of focus away from Gothic conventions to psychological realism defines *St. Leon* as a fundamentally different type of narrative. Possession of the philosopher's stone has left Reginald wholly preoccupied with "experiments and lucubrations" that, like Faust's pact with Mephistopheles, have conferred infernal, superhuman powers: "While I was busied with my crucible, I was able more vividly to present to myself my seeming superiority to the rest of my species." Godwin describes Reginald's megalomania and alienation from the rest of humanity in a scene reminiscent of Faust's soliloquy in the cave:

> I had felt that the wealth of the whole world was at my disposal and that I held my life by a tenure independent and imperial. These are not the class of conceptions that fade and perish from the mind. We cannot wake from them as from a dream, and forget that ever such things were. They have changed the whole constitution of *my* nature. It would have required a miracle, greater than all the consecrated legends of our church record, to have restored me to what I formerly was. (II: 248)

Reginald's exilic wandering and spiritual separation from the human family also suggest parallels with the atonement earned by Faust and Byron's Manfred. The resulting sense of isolation perceived by the empathic reader is intensified by Godwin's profound identification with his protagonist. As Hazlitt observes in *The Spirit of the Age*, "[o]ur author takes a given subject from nature or form books, and then fills it up with the ardent workings of his own mind, with the teeming and audible pulses of his own heart. The work (so to speak) and the author are one" —that is, the novel presents a drama of Godwin's inner life. (XX: 25) There is also an intriguing parallelism between the alchemist's transmutation of base metals into gold and the novelist's conversion of human experience into symbolic form. Employed as forces for the relief of human suffering the philosopher's stone and *elixir vitae* objectify the principles of *Political Justice*. Godwin, the philosophical novelist is, like Reginald, a reluctant sorcerer; as agents of inexplicable powers the radical thinker and the alchemist suffer persecution—the latter because he cannot explain to anyone's satisfaction how he suddenly becomes rich; the former because in *Political Justice* Godwin challenges the arbitrary power of government with the divine authority of reason.

By means of a ruse Reginald is lured to Gabor's castle, which is situated in a gloomy romantic landscape. Unlike his previous jailers, Gabor is not susceptible to petty or even massive bribery; he covets the philosopher's stone and initiation into the secrets of eternal life. Possessing "all the ingredients of sublimity" and "the ingredients of heroic virtue," Gabor is Ferdinando Falkland's [villain and persecutor of Caleb Williams in the eponymous novel] double and another representative of chivalry whose misanthropy is the inversion of the code by which he had once vowed to govern his conduct. (IV: 201) The mistake Reginald makes is to assume that the philosopher's stone is solely reserved "for beneficent purposes," that to such alone "it is consecrated." (IV: 183) Gabor would use this power to feed his misanthropy and punish mankind.

In the face of such intransigence only a *deus ex machina* can save Reginald and, remarkably enough, deliverance arrives in an army led by his now mature son. The reader learns that Charles de

St. Leon has for some time been hunting for his father in order to make good on his promised revenge. In the meantime, he has sufficiently recaptured the family honor and his father's former status; as a knight riding under the banner of the Holy Roman Empire he has recently fought in the climactic siege of Szigetvar (1566) in which the sultan himself was killed and Hungary was liberated. Rumors of unexplained wealth and boundless charity lead him across Central Europe to the threshold of Gabor's castle, to which he lays siege. In the ensuing battle and bombardment, the massive structure is levelled, and Gabor goes down fighting. Reginald is discovered in the smoldering ruins and brought before his rescuer, whom he recognizes as his son. On account of his new, youthful appearance, engineered by a quick dose of the *elixir vitae*, Reginald is not recognized as the notorious Sieur de Chantillon, his alias as the "saviour of Hungary." Instead, Charles takes him for an innocent victim of Gabor's treachery and, in his new disguise as the young nobleman D'Aubigny, Reginald is invited to live as the friend and confidant of his son. In a letter from Charles, he learns the young man's most intimate secret:

> Magic dissolves the whole principle and arrangement of human action, subverts all generous enthusiasm and dignity, and renders life itself loathsome and intolerable. I had a father whom I . . . . loved: he became the dupe of these infernal arts. I had a mother, the paragon of the creation: that father murdered her. All the anguish I ever felt, has derived its source from alchemy and magic. (IV: 325)

He also learns of his son's love for Pandora, the daughter of the Palatine of Hungary, and agrees to serve as his go-between. Unfortunately, D'Aubigny (Reginald) finds favor with the young woman, arousing the jealousy of Charles who, in keeping with the code of chivalry, challenges his new friend to a duel. After a heartfelt colloquy in which all confusion is resolved, the novel closes with Reginald's proud observation that his son has realized the chivalric ideal and established the basis for earthly happiness:

> I was the hero's father—but no! I am not blinded by paternal partiality;—
> but no! he was indeed what I thought him, as near the climax of dignity and
> virtue as the frailty of our nature will admit. His virtue was at length
> crowned with the most enviable reward the earth has to boast, the faithful
> attachment of a noble-minded and accomplished woman. I am happy to
> close my eventful and melancholy story with so pleasing a termination.
> Whatever may have been the result of my personal experience of human life,
> I can never recollect the fate of Charles and Pandora without confessing with
> exultation, that this busy and anxious world of ours yet contains something
> in its stores that is worth living for. (IV: 478)

In narrating his Promethean sufferings, Reginald does not seek vindication for his "vices and follies"; he presents his travels as a warning to others to avoid the temptations of black magic.

Many critics, starting with Leslie Stephen in the late nineteenth century, have compared *St. Leon* to Voltaire's *Candide* (1759)
and Samuel Johnson's *Rasselas* (1759), citing Godwin's novel as a
prototype of the *Bildungsroman*.[6] On the surface, Godwin's novel
does seem to present travel as a process of *Bildung* or character development but actually represents, as in *Candide* and *Rasselas*, a protagonist formed by disillusionment rather than fostered by growth-
enhancing experiences. Formally, too, as Percy G. Adams suggests,
"travel literature as education, as a means of structuring experience, is very close to the bildungsroman." (188) However, in contrast to *Rasselas* or the prototype of the genre, Goethe's *Wilhelm
Meister* (1777), *St. Leon* is fundamentally an anti-*Bildungsroman*, its
protagonist an anti-*Bildungsheld*, and his journey a dark parody or
inverse of the *Bildungsreise*. Like Goethe's Wilhelm, who develops
from actor to physician, Reginald seeks to acquire social usefulness
in a disordered world. But the enabling knowledge, the special gift

---

6   Leslie Stephen, "William Godwin's Novels," in *Studies of a Biographer*, second
series (London: G.P. Putnam's Sons, 1902), Vol. III, 119–154. See also P.N. Furbank, "Godwin's Novels," *Essays in Criticism* 5 (July 1955): 214–228; George
Sherburn, "Godwin's Later Novels," *Studies in Romanticism* I (1962): 65–82;
Wallace A. Flanders, "Godwin and Gothicism: St. Leon," *Texas Studies in Literature and Language* 8 (1976): 533–545; Dean T. Hughes, *Romance and Psychological
Realism in William Godwin's Novels* (New York: Arno Press, 1980).

he acquires, according to the conventional paradigm of *Bildung*, is completely false, a sleight of hand. In contrast to Wilhelm's choice of medicine as his vocation, Reginald's practice of alchemy is an inversion of medicine; it is a travesty of healing, for it does not repair but destroys the fabric of society and leads to even more suffering. To the starving citizens of Budapest, he offers charity without giving them the ability to help themselves. Moreover, unlike Rasselas's venture beyond the Happy Valley, Reginald's *Bildungsreise* is not undertaken as a deliberate effort to learn through experience but, in a manner reminiscent of Felix Krull—Thomas Mann's parodistic *Bildungsheld*—the initial journey from Paris to Lake Constance, and all subsequent travel, is motivated by financial embarrassment, the stain of dishonor, the pressure of creditors and lawmen. (Any personal development that takes place en route is purely adventitious and not the product of Reginald's agency or willed behavior.) Finally, Godwin departs from the *Bildungsroman* pattern in two essential ways: first, ultimate wisdom is attained not as the result of trials of character but through the intervention of the supernatural; secondly, disillusionment is not a vehicle for Reginald's reintegration into society, but rather leads to his permanent exile from the human community. Finally, the confirmation of Reginald's identity as an anti-*Bildungsheld* emerges at the terminus of his wanderings where we find him incapable of undertaking significant action.

As we have seen, Godwin's interest in travel writing does not end at the borders of Europe; the process of transposition, of selecting and adopting details from one context to another, is also exemplified in his treatment of Reginald's encounter with the East in Turkish-dominated Hungary, especially in confrontations between the supernatural traveler and the sultan's representative, the bashaw. Godwin's interest in the Near East is anticipated or fed by Lady Mary Wortley Montagu's *Turkish Letters* (published in 1763), Johnson's *Rasselas*, and the long tradition of the Oriental Tale in England. In turn, *St. Leon* anticipates by a few decades the

Orientalism of Thomas De Quincey, Lord Byron, and Eugène Delacroix (1798–1863). That William Godwin represents Reginald's efforts to aid the starving population of Budapest as a presumptuous, insensitive act suggests parallels with the colonization or invasion of the east by western armies and values. There are also parallels between the incursion of Reginald into the east and space travel as depicted in a popular seventeenth-century narrative of an extraordinary voyage, *Man in the Moone* (1638), written by Godwin's namesake, the Bishop Francis Godwin (1562–1633). But despite such resemblances, the French protagonist of *St. Leon* does not roam the surface of the moon or the American wilderness; he explores, instead, the inner psyche of Europe and probes its margins of darkness, a region still plunged in darkness in the late twentieth century—darkness issuing from long-simmering tribal and religious feuds.

Another useful approach to *St. Leon* is to compare it to other works seeking to define the language and content suitable to the novel, such as William Congreve's Preface to his novel *Incognita* (1691) or Eliza Haywood's *Idalia* in volume III of *Secret Histories, Novels, and Poems* (1734). Godwin's presentation of the supernatural is a central theme of "romance," according to Congreve, who distinguishes between the novel and the romance based on the presence of the fantastic—"heroes, lofty language, miraculous contingencies, and impossible performances"—over "more familiar" subject matter. But Haywood has no such qualms about conflating the categories of "novel" and "romance" in describing *Idalia* as a novel, even though it includes elements of ancient Greek romance.[7]

One of the most intriguing self-reflexive formal features of *St. Leon* is its setting in the sixteenth century, the era of the novel's emergence as a fully self-standing genre in England. This is a

---

7   My quotations from Congreve and Haywood are from Percy G. Adams, *Travel Literature and the Evolution of the Novel* (Lexington, Kentucky: University Press of Kentucky, 1983), 7.

striking example of the way in which a Romantic artifact mediates cultural phenomena of the past as well as other traditions and in this way offers clues to its own interpretation. Godwin incorporates an additional dimension of historical significance to the layers of generic diversity provided by the conventions of travel, romance, and the *Bildungsroman*. Generating typological analogies between the ideological conflicts in the sixteenth and in the eighteenth centuries, he suggests that alchemy symbolizes a rival, subversive epistemological system which is analogous to capitalism and empiricism as a worldview and a means of social organization. Like alchemy, capitalism offers a self-enclosed, self-sufficient system of economics and governance, not dependent on the hegemonic relationships fostered by feudalism and autocracy. Situated on the margins of the canon, *St. Leon* displays an impressive command of psychology, and the persecution and martyrdom of the protagonist is a poignant reminder of Godwin's fate as a prophet of peaceful social and political revolution in an age of reaction.

Contemporary travel literature presents variations on Godwin's fusion of elements of the Gothic, romance, and the *Bildungsroman* coupled with *vrai* or *vraisemblable* representations of foreign cultures as well as historical stagecraft. Some examples of travel writing that depict Europe in an age of transition include the following texts by friends or acquaintances, many of whom congregated at Joseph Johnson's bookshop: Thomas Holcroft's translation of the *Memoirs of the Freiherr von der Trenck* (1788) and his own *Travels from Hamburg, through Westphalia, Holland, and the Netherlands* (1804); Mary Wollstonecraft's *A Short Residence in Sweden* (1796); Arthur Young's *Travels in France* (1792); Helen Maria Williams's *Letters from France* (1790); and Samuel Taylor Coleridge's *Satyrane's Letters* (written 1798–99 and published in 1809 in *The Friend*). These texts offer observations on European culture and society in the wake of the French Revolution—observations that are imbued with an emergent new sensibility which is openly in sympathy with radical politics and social change. Another possible source for

Godwin's familiarity with details of topography, architecture, and local customs throughout the length and breadth of Reginald's travels is Johann Georg Keyssler's *Travels through Germany, Bohemia, Hungary, Switzerland, Italy, and Lorraine* (1740; English translation published in 1756–57). Reginald's progress through Europe duplicates Keyssler's itinerary almost exactly. This is just one key to appreciating Godwin's method of adapting or transposing material (including generic conventions) from one context (travel/history) to another (fiction); this process of transposition might without exaggeration be described as the definitive creative activity of the Romantic Age.

The most sustained example of transposition on Godwin's model is found in Ann Radcliffe's use of her sources in the novels *The Romance of the Forest* (1791), *The Mysteries of Udolfo* (1794), and *The Italian* (1797). Radcliffe's main sources for French and Italian scenery, from which she borrowed freely, are Ramond de Carbonniére's descriptions of the Pyrenees and Gascony, Salvator Rosa's landscape paintings, and Pierre-Jean Grosley's *New Observations on Italy and Its Inhabitants* (translated into English in 1769). Another variety of travel writing offering suggestive correspondences with Godwin's mediation of foreign cultures depicts foreign observers offering piquant first-hand commentary on other countries. A popular and widely practiced genre in the eighteenth century, some of the most influential examples include George Psalmanazar's *A Description of Formosa* (1704), Montesquieu's *Lettres persanes* (1721), Lord George Lyttleton's *Letters from a Persian in England* (1735), J.B. Haldé's *Description de la Chine* (1738), Françoise de Graffigny's *Lettres d'une Peruvienne* (1747; translated into English in 1748), and Oliver Goldsmith's *Citizen of the World* (1762). These texts must be distinguished from novels with foreign settings, such as Aphra Behn's *Oroonoko* (1688), Daniel Defoe's *Moll Flanders* (1721), Antoine François Prévost's *Manon Lescaut* (1731), Arthur Young's *The Adventures of Emmera; or the Fair American* (1767), as well as more contemporary examples, such as Charlotte Smith's *The Old Manor House*

(1793), M.G. Lewis's *The Monk* (1796), François-René Chateaubriand's *Atala* (1801) and *René* (1802), and the novels by Radcliffe mentioned above. There is an older tradition of travel writing that provides additional resonance for Godwin's fusion of genres. These texts include Plato's *Republic*, Thomas More's *Utopia* (1516), Francis Bacon's *New Atlantis* (1627), and Jonathan Swift's *Gulliver's Travels* (1726), which, despite its near contemporaneity, belongs by form and affinity to this group.

Combined with the travel motif the novel's historical setting reveals another major objective of the text: to allegorize a shift in epistemological paradigms. Godwin situates this transitional moment near the close of the sixteenth century and Reginald de St. Leon, alchemist and knight, is representative of an epistemological system—alchemy as a forerunner and rival to modern science—and a social system—feudalism—that are both on the brink of obsolescence. Reginald is thus an anachronism on multiple levels—as a member of warrior class dispossessed of its function in society and as an adept in an inferior science that is rapidly becoming marginalized. As Godwin's protagonist carries alchemy and feudalism up to the threshold of the age of science and capitalism his travels afford a broad overview of European culture during this transitional, crisis-ridden period in history. His travels coincide in large part with the *Bildungsreise* of the sixteenth century's last important alchemist, Paracelsus (né Theophrastus von Hohenheim) whose wanderings in pursuit of knowledge and converts took him from Switzerland across Germany, the modern-day Czech Republic and Slovakia to Hungary. Opposition to Paracelsus's teachings in Western Europe suggests the intolerance of alchemy in the homeland of Renaissance science. Reginald's persecution by the Spanish Inquisition and in Hungary by the Turks reflects a different kind of intolerant jealousy on the part of autocratic authority toward a rival superstition.

The interpretative pattern Godwin imposes on intellectual history—the transition from alchemy to modern science—is perhaps more accessible to the modern reader in three analogous descriptions of the sixteenth and seventeenth centuries as a transitional period for the literary-scientific sensibility found in the writings by Hugo von Hofmannsthal (1874–1929), T.S. Eliot (1888–1965), and Michel Foucault (1926–1984). In his essay on "The Metaphysical Poets" Eliot famously characterizes a crisis that he perceives in European culture as a consequence of a "dissociation of sensibility" in poetry:

> It is something which had happened to the mind of England between the time of Donne or Lord Herbert of Cherbury and the time of Tennyson or Browning; it is the difference between the intellectual poet and the reflective poet. Tennyson and Browning are poets, and they think; but they do not feel their thought as immediately as the odour of a rose. A thought to Donne was an experience; it modified his sensibility.[8]

In the "Letter of Lord Chandos" Hofmannsthal offers a fictionalized account of the crisis outlined by Eliot. In a letter dated 1603 the poet Lord Philip Chandos apologizes to his patron, Francis Bacon, for giving up all his remaining literary projects. After struggling for two years to write, he admits to the irretrievable loss of his poetic sensibility. In phrasing remarkably similar to Eliot's, Chandos reminisces about the organic unity of all experience and perception that he once possessed in abundance but is now gone:

> When in my hunting lodge I drank the warm foaming milk which an unkempt wretch had drained into a wooden pail from the udder of a beautiful gentle-eyed cow, the sensation was no different from that which I experienced when, seated on a bench built into the window of my study, my mind absorbed the sweet and foaming nourishment from a book. The one was like the other: neither was superior to the other, whether in dreamlike celestial quality or in physical intensity—and thus it prevailed through the whole expanse of life in all directions.[9]

---

8   T.S. Eliot, "The Metaphysical Poets" (1921), *Selected Prose of T.S. Eliot.* Ed. Frank Kermode (New York: Harcourt, Brace, Jovanovich, 1975), 64.

9   Hugo Hofmannsthal, "The Letter of Lord Chandos." *Selected Prose of Hugo von Hofmannsthal,* ed. and trans. Mary Hottinger and Tania and James Stern (London: Routledge and Kegan Paul, 1952), 132.

Along with Eliot and Hofmannsthal, Foucault, too, suggests that the seventeenth century "marks" an essential divide in the intellectual life of Europe, from "the disappearance of the old superstitious or magical beliefs and the entry of nature, at long last, into the scientific order." He describes the transformation that Godwin represents in the vicissitudes of his suffering protagonist as the transition from sign and social systems based on credulous or naive empiricism to ones based on idealism and rationalism; from mental operations based on comparison to discrimination; from similitude to difference. *St. Leon* may therefore be seen as a vehicle for representing an ideological conflict which was "of the greatest consequence for Western thought . . . . [T]he empirical domain which sixteenth-century man saw as a complex of kinships, resemblances, and affinities, and in which language and things were endlessly interwoven—this whole vast field was to take on a new configuration."[10]

Godwin's thwarting of the generic expectations of travel fiction, the Gothic novel, romance, and the *Bildungsroman* in *St. Leon* has confounded readers and critics for two centuries. Similarly, few critics have been receptive to his interpretation of intellectual history. Most expected in each succeeding novel a performance closer to *Caleb Williams* with its more conventional setting in the English countryside and its more accessible tropes of persecution, flight, and criminal detection. The effects of generic fusion are compounded by Godwin's experiment with archaic diction that at times approaches pastiche, which may provide the novel with an additional layer of authenticity but does so at the cost of distancing readers accustomed to a less alienating linguistic texture. The defeat of these expectations is, however, offset by the incorporation of other generic elements, including those kinds of long narrative fiction identified by Northrup Frye—the romance, the confession, and the anatomy—as well as several other modes, including historical, didactic, pastoral, travel, Gothic, and Orientalist fiction. The generic

---

10   Michel Foucault, *The Order of Things* (New York: Vintage Books, 1973), 54.

diversity on display in *St. Leon* reflects the encyclopedic appropriation and syncretic mixing and fusing of literary genres and literary modes associated with Friedrich Schlegel's definition of "romantische Poesie." Such generic diversity also affirms Henry James's definition of the novel as "the most independent, the most elastic, most prodigious of literary form."[11]

---

11   Henry James, *Art of the Novel* (New York: Charles Scribner's Sons, 1934), 326.

9 From Translation to Authorship: Anglophone Women Writers and Goethe

> "One great acquisition you have infallibly made: the acqui-
> sition of a Teacher and a Prophet for yourself! Alone of men,
> very far beyond all other men, Goethe seems to me to have
> understood his Century . . . . Such a man is as a Prometheus,
> who in time of midnight and specters miraculously brings
> fire and light out of Heaven itself."
>
> *Thomas Carlyle to John Sullivan Dwight, 29 December 1836*

Johann Wolfgang von Goethe (1749–1832) is the central figure in the German literary canon. Poet, novelist, playwright, and scientist, Goethe is to the German language what William Shakespeare (1564–1616) is to English-speaking cultures, only more so. The fact that such a protean, polymathic, and "great" figure should have emerged on the doorstep of the modern world, rather than in a faraway era, makes Goethe feel less mythical, more like a contemporary, and more like one of us. Indeed, Goethe spoke and composed his works in what is recognizably modern German instead of a dialect that requires training to grasp, even for native speakers, as is the case when students approach Shakespeare's Elizabethan English for the first time.

From the early nineteenth century onward Goethe served as an Anglo-American sage and literary icon. His popularity exceeded that of British and American authors. Thomas Carlyle (1795–1881), the Scottish historian, essayist, and critic, served as the chief advocate for the adoption of Goethe as a role model for aspiring writers in early Victorian Britain. By reading Goethe's life experiences and personality as exemplary and worthy of emulation, in his early writings Carlyle established a pattern that came to dominate British and American cultural life throughout the second half of the nineteenth century. In the diverse and fascinating body of Carlyle's critical writing and translations textual exegesis plays an unexpectedly minor role. In its place a full-blown cult of personality materializes along with a blueprint for an ideology of hero worship that becomes more fully mapped out in the cultural and political life of twentieth-century Europe and twenty-first century America and, again, Europe.

It is a curious feature of the transmission of foreign cultures in anglophone countries that Goethe's reputation was not, in contrast to parallel processes in Russia or France, formed by appropriating or resisting such major works as the lyrical *The Sorrows of Young Werther* (1774) or the magisterial *Faust* (1808 and 1832). Instead, Goethe's reputation among speakers of English grew out of the controversy surrounding his personality, ethics, and character. From the publication of the first English translation of *Werther* in 1780 to the appearance of Carlyle's translation of *Wilhelm Meister's Apprenticeship* in 1824, criticism of Goethe in Britain and North America was inflected by a series of conflicting interpretations focused not on readings of these and other works—at least not in the sense indicated by Coleridge's "practical criticism"—but, quite differently, on what George Saintsbury, in his reappraisal of Goethe's impact on Victorian critics, derided as "anthropological" interpretations or pre-Freudian probings of the authorial psyche as well as moral judgments which were inferred from the text and then projected back onto the author.[1]

The biographical impulse in Carlyle's criticism was in fact assimilated from Goethe's own reflections on literature and his practice as a critic. In *Gespräche mit Goethe* [*Conversations with Goethe*] (1836 and 1848), for example, Johann Peter Eckermann notes the poet's assertion that

> Personality is everything in art and poetry, yet there are many weak personages among the modern critics who do not admit this, but look upon a great personality in a work of poetry or art merely as a kind of trifling appendage. However, to feel and respect a great personality one must be something oneself.[2]

---

1   George Saintsbury, *A History of Criticism and Literary Taste in Europe* (Edinburgh and London: William Blackwood and Sons, 1900–1904), Vol. III, 495.

2   Entry for 13 February 1831 in *Goethe's Gespräche, 1831–32*, ed. Woldemar Freiherr von Biedermann (Leipzig: Biedermann, 1890), Vol. VIII, 15.

A perusal of the *Gespräche mit Goethe*, the collected *Briefe*, and all of Goethe's criticism confirms that he only rarely discusses a specific work and its literary characteristics; instead, his interest in the writer's personality nearly always supercedes textual analysis or an explicit discussion of aesthetic qualities. Thus, not only does Goethe validate a critical method or hermeneutic based on reading authorial personality, deciphering the allegorical value of a poet's personality emerges as one of the chief organizing principles in the cultural life of nineteenth-century Europe. The critical response to Goethe displayed in the work of Germaine de Staël (1766–1817) and Hyppolyte Taine (1828–1893), Heinrich Heine (1797–1856) and other writers associated with the *Jungdeutschland* ["Young Germany"] literary movement, along with Carlyle and his disciples in Britain, suggests the scope of Goethe's impact on European intellectuals in a pivotal age.

As displaced intellectuals, British dissenters and Jacobin supporters of the French Revolution, like their American counterparts in and around Cambridge, Massachusetts, each representing the strictest subsets of Puritan social subdivisions, formed the basis of "oppositional" culture in their respective countries. Bound by religious heritage and the shared experience of pilgrimage for the sake of intellectual and spiritual enrichment, the British mediators of German culture were, however, divided from their Boston cousins by differences in class and social influence. In nineteenth-century New England, descendants of the original Puritans were socially dominant and headed up the central institutions of local culture, such as the Unitarian Church and Harvard College. In Britain, by contrast, Dissenters from the Anglican majority, Scots Presbyterians, and other sectarians were politically and socially marginalized, as were women, Roman Catholics, and Jews. Nonetheless, members of all these peripheral groups formed the nucleus of the German-trained intelligentsia in Britain and the United States.

Moreover, the mediatory publications of these outsiders, chiefly translations and criticism, cast a spotlight on the integral relationship between the interpretation of Goethe's works and the intense effort underway in the first half of the nineteenth century to declare America's cultural independence from Great Britain. At the same time, the mediation of German literature, above all the writings of Goethe, arrives as a vehicle enabling the migration of women writers form the margins of cultural life to the center. Indeed, the efforts of Margaret Fuller (1810–1850) to critique and translate German literature and her emergence as one of the most important literary figures of the time are inseparable. The arc of her career is similar to that of other Anglophone women writers such as Mary Wollstonecraft (1759–1797), Sarah Austin (1793–1867), George Eliot (1819–1880), and Edith Wharton (1862–1937), namely, a prosthetic relationship between the translation and reviewing of German literature as mediators evolved from "pre-writing" and "re-writing" phases of literary development to "writing" as the creators of original works of criticism and of the imagination.

Mary Wollstonecraft

The popularity and impact of British literature in German-speaking countries—such as the formative connection between Anglophilia and the Enlightenment in Germany—has been well-documented.[3] But unlike the situation in Germany, where admiration of all things British historically has been and remains a vital presence in intellectual life, there has traditionally been strong resistance by many scholars and critics of British literature to accept a model of cultural history that acknowledges the impact of the transmission of German literature and thought has had on shaping British cultural identity. This may have had something to do with the fact that women and other cultural outsiders played leading roles as cultural intermediaries, and their mediating activities also constituted

---

3   See, for example, Michael Maurer, *Aufklärung und Anglophilie in Deutschland* (Göttingen und Zürich: Vandenhoeck und Ruprecht, 1987), 41–106.

political acts that not only reflected sympathy with Continental ideologies and revolutions, but also initiated their journeys from the margins of literary culture to the center. Also underpinning resistance to the work of marginalized cultural intermediaries is the traditional paradigm of literary history, according to which the processes of cultural production that threaten to demote or weaken the iconic position of the author, and reveal the institutional root system of canonical works, are erased or ignored.

In order to restore this underlying root system, much of the original writing generated by friends and admirers of William Godwin—whose bookshop formed the center of radical (i.e., "liberal" in the American sense) resistance to the authoritarian suppression and censorship of dissent by the British government in the wake of the French Revolution (1789–1799)—must be viewed in the context of the mediating activity of Henry Fuseli, Mary Wollstonecraft, Thomas Holcroft, and William Taylor. Like William Godwin, Fuseli (1741–1825) was originally trained to be a minister, but in the liberal Protestant Zwinglian sect. However, he quickly abandoned that vocation in favor of a career as a painter and author. Like Wollstonecraft (with whom he was romantically involved before she met Godwin), Fuseli passed through phases of enthusiasm for and subsequent disillusionment with the fellow Swiss Jean-Jacques Rousseau (1712–1778). After arriving in London in 1760, Fuseli led an ambitious campaign to introduce the cultural riches of the German language to Britain, publishing the first English translation of J. J. Winckelmann's *Geschichte der Kunst des Alterthums* [*The History of the Art of Antiquity*] in 1764—a work with which Goethe himself was deeply engaged and which was deeply influential in the decades to come. With the encouragement of his intimate friend, the publisher Joseph Johnson (1738–1809), Fuseli began to publish reviews of leading German writers, such as Kotzebue, Wieland, Schiller, and Goethe. He also wrote the first history of German literature in English, which was unfortunately lost in a fire in 1770. Fuseli was thus better positioned than anyone before Henry Crabb Robinson and

Samuel Taylor Coleridge to interpret German literature for anglo-phone readers.

The charismatic Fuseli attracted disciples, and none was more important as a cultural intermediary in her own right than Wollstonecraft. Her intense and prolonged engagement with German culture suggests the need to reassess the traditional attribution of some eighty reviews of German books published in *The Analytical Review* (one of the leading radical journals of the time), including notable reviews of Goethe's dramas *Stella* (1806) and *Clavigo* (1774), and possibly to transfer several of them to Wollstonecraft's author-ship. For example, the seven reviews of German works (such as John Armstrong's 1790 translation of Goethe's novel *Werther*—reti-tled *The Confidential Letters of Albert; from his first attachment to Char-lotte to her death*) in the *Analytical* assigned to Wollstonecraft by Mar-ilyn Butler seems an insufficient number considering Wollstone-craft's unusually strong competence in German and the remarkable frequency with which German works were reviewed in its pages—a workload beyond the capacity of a single writer.[4]

Wollstonecraft's major achievement as a translator from Ger-man appeared in 1790. *Elements of Morality for the use of children* was freely adapted from the German text by Christian Gotthilf Salz-mann (1744–1811), an influential writer on education. Salzmann's importance was noted by Goethe and others at the time and his *Moralisches Elementarbuch* was reprinted throughout the nineteenth century. Indeed, the 1785 edition was reissued as recently as 1980. Wollstonecraft's *Elements of Morality* is not a mechanical translation or mere hackwork. On the contrary, it represents a pathbreaking exercise in transposing a foreign text into a domesticated form for British readers. There are strong ideological and stylistic ligatures binding *Elements of Morality* to Wollstonecraft's original works of a pedagogical and didactic character, including *Thoughts on the*

Education of Daughters (1787), *Mary: A Fiction* (1788), *The Wrongs of Woman, or Maria* (1798), *The Female Reader* (1789), and, of course, the seminal *A Vindication of the Rights of Woman* (1790). Moreover, Wollstonecraft's novel *Young Grandison* (1790) is also, like *Elements of Morality*, essentially a reworking of a foreign text. In this case, the appropriated work is *De kleine Grandison* (1782), a novel by the Dutch writer Margaretha Maria Geertruid de Cambon-van de Werken (1734–1796), which was itself an adaptation of Samuel Richardson's original published in 1754. Such interconnections between Wollstonecraft's writings published as original work and her translations anticipated the instrumental function that the transmission of German culture served in the careers of women writers in Britain and America, including Sarah Austin (1793–1867), Margaret Fuller, and George Eliot (1819–1880).

Sarah Austin and Margaret Fuller

Sarah Austin was an uncannily accomplished translator who elevated Goethe to the status of the "strong poet" with whom Anglo-American writers grappled from the 1780s to the middle of the nineteenth century. It was her translation of various first-hand accounts of encounters with Goethe, entitled *Characteristics of Goethe from the German of Falk, Von Müller and others* (1833), that fed the British reading public's burgeoning appetite for any contact with the object of the cult of personality which was initiated by Carlyle a few years earlier. In 1841 Austin published another influential text, *Fragments of German Prose Writers*, which contains extensive notes on the texts and over one hundred pages of background information on the authors selected for the anthology. The notes and authors' profiles embody a prescient attempt to articulate the canon of German non-verse forms and the work of women writers, such as Bettina (née Brentano) von Arnim (1785–1859), Caroline de la Motte Fouqué (1773–1831), Ida Gräfin von Hahn-Hahn (1805–1880), Louisa Queen of Prussia (1776–1810), Rahel Varnhagen von Ense

162 CHILDREN OF PROMETHEUS

(1771–1833), and Johanna Schopenhauer (1766–1838). In 1854 *Austin published Germany from 1760 to 1814*, an original study of German culture, manners, and institutions, which appeared contemporaneously with "The Natural History of German Life" (1854), one of George Eliot's most insightful publications on German culture.[5]

Just three years after its initial publication in Germany, Margaret Fuller's translation of *Eckermann's Conversations with Goethe* appeared in 1839. Her translation is accompanied by the first lengthy critical biography of Goethe in *any* language, in which Fuller seeks to distance herself from the partisan politics of Goethe's reception in the English-speaking world. Fuller offers a vision of the direction that American literary criticism should take going forward:

> I am not fanatical as to benefits to be derived from the study of German Literature. I suppose, indeed, that there lie the life and learning of the century, and that he who does not go these sources can have no just notion of the workings of the spirit of the European world these last fifty years or more . . .[6]

Fuller was strongly attracted to Goethe's imaginative writings ("of German writers [Goethe is] the most English and the most Greek"), even if she expressed qualms concerning details of his personal life. After the *Conversations* she translated Goethe's verse drama *Torquato Tasso* (1790) about a 16th-century Italian writer who goes mad. This play was included in the posthumously published collection of her work—*Art, Literature and the Drama* (1869). Fuller also translated *Die Günderode* (1840), the fictionalized correspondence between the German Romantic poets Bettina von Arnim and Karoline von Günderrode (1780–1806). In the translator's preface, Fuller explains why she was drawn to this work of extraordinary emotional intimacy and cultural insight:

---

5   Review essay of the first two parts of Wilhelm Riehl's *Naturgeschichte des Volkes als Grundlage einer deutschen Social-Politik* (1851 and 1854).

6   *Conversations with Goethe in the Last Years of His Life (1839)*, trans. Margaret Fuller (Boston: James Munroe and Company, 1857), xvii.

And not only are these letters interesting as presenting this view of the interior of German life, and of an ideal relation realized, but the high state of culture in Germany which presented to the thoughts of those women themes of poesy and philosophy as readily, as to the English or American girl come the choice of a dress, the last concert or assembly, has made them expressions of the noblest aspirations, filled them with thoughts and oftentimes deep thoughts on the great subjects.[7]

In the conclusion to her translator's preface to the *Conversations*, Fuller notes that the remarkable explosion of cultural activity in Germany over the previous eighty-five years was directly related to the "transfusion of such energies as are manifested in Goethe, Kant, and Schelling, into these private lives." And she considers the emulation of Germany's great poets and philosophers, "a creation not less worthy of our admiration than the forms which the Muse has given them to bestow on the world through the immediate working of their chosen means. These are not less the children of the genius than his statue or the exposition of this method."[8]

Even more notable is an essay simply entitled "Goethe," which was written in 1835 and published in another posthumous collection of Fuller's writings, *Life Within and Without* (1860). Here Fuller offers guidelines for a typological interpretation of the German poet's life for readers who accepted him as their cultural savior. Regarding the famous "Bruchstücke" passage in Goethe's autobiography, *From my Life: Poetry and Truth* (1831), she validates the confessional dimension of Goethe's writings:

> *Faust* contains the great idea of his life, as indeed there is but one great poetic idea possible to man, the progress of a soul through the various forms of existence. All his other works . . . are mere chapters to this poem. . . . *Faust*, had it been completed in the spirit in which was begun, would have been the *Divina Commedia* of its age.[9]

---

7   *Günderode*, trans. Margaret Fuller and Minna Wesselhoft (Boston: T.O.H.P. Burnham, 1861), x.

8   *Ibid.*, xi.

9   Margaret Fuller Ossoli, *Life Within and Without*, ed. Arthur B. Fuller (Boston: Brown, Taggard and Chase, 1860), 35.

Fuller's essay was merely the germ of a planned full-scale biography, which would have pre-dated G.H. Lewes's *Life of Goethe* (1855), the first work of its kind in any language, by two decades. The loss to American literature and to the interpretation of Goethe, when Fuller drowned in a shipwreck in 1850, is incalculable.

Importing Goethe and German culture into New England, as Fuller did, answered a deep-seated need for greater worldliness and personal growth that could only be achieved along an axis of confrontation between what is familiar and what is foreign to the anglophone self. The widespread appropriation of German cultural paradigms offered a short cut to acquiring intellectual capital by a young, culturally voracious nation. For Margaret Fuller and her fellow mediators in New England, the encounter with the great, compelling example of Goethe was inseparable from their quest for author's laurels of their own as well as the creation of a uniquely American literary identity separate from that of Great Britain. However, as enriching and enabling as the cultural riches of Germany proved to be, their transmission proved disruptive to the status quo in New England, regardless of whether one stood for institutional innovation and greater openness or for tradition and less permeable borders. The educational reforms promoted by Harvard students who had studied in Germany and met Goethe in Weimar threatened to subvert the established hierarchies of cultural authority by equipping the younger generation with potent new methodologies that facilitated cultural critique and functioned, in early twenty-first century terms, analogously to poststructuralist or neo-Marxist theory. Even though the German literary dispensation was abundant and various, the herald of this triumphant invasion was Goethe. Evidence for this is found in the many anglophone books, periodicals, and speeches that assigned cultural leadership to him. As the principal German author who formed the chief threat to the ideological hegemony of the Puritan old guard and the institutions they dominated, Goethe, and one's attitude toward him, became a litmus test for cultural politics in New England.

The danger that German literary invasion posed to the stability of the establish cultural order in New England was, in fact, genuine. The ideas spawned in Weimar, Jena, and Göttingen were not the products of a society moving towards a popular democracy like the United States. They were, instead, ideas nourished by aristocratic patronage mechanisms in an authoritarian (and anachronistic) feudal monarchy that was highly invested in the assertion of German cultural particularity in defiance of French cultural and political domination of Western Europe. It is indeed paradoxical that an American literary movement like Transcendentalism should have been shaped, in large part, by the emulation of Goethe, an ennobled cultural hero who made no secret of his indifference or even hostility to emerging democratic institutions.

Ralph Waldo Emerson (1803–1882) found Goethe's aristocratic sensibility difficult to reconcile with his admiration for the great poet's writings. As we have seen, the code word used by antagonistic critics as well as ambivalent admirers was Goethe's "morality," which was, of course, deemed inseparable from his reputation as the supreme literary artist of the age. This identification suggested an awareness of a conflict between the values of New England society, which was built on a Puritan religious and ethical foundation, and the dominant cultural movement emerging in Germany, which was modeled on the aesthetic life personally embodied by Goethe. The problem confronted by Emerson and Fuller was paradoxical: how were they to engender an American cultural revolution devoted to individual development based on an imported aristocratic aestheticism when, by contrast, the civil society of New England was founded on Puritan collectivism, Christian self-abnegation, and egalitarian ethics? Emerson's ambivalence was ultimately overcome as evidenced by the publication of the essay "Goethe, or, the Writer" in *Representative Men* (1850).

George Eliot

The anglophone writer whose achievement is most closely associated with Goethe is George Eliot (1819–1880). In 1854, on the eve of her scandalous elopement to Germany with the still married George Henry Lewes, Marian Evans had not yet adopted her famous pen name or published her first work of fiction. What she had accomplished, however, was not inconsiderable. Even if, with the publication of *Middlemarch* in 1871–72, she had not proven herself to be the preeminent Victorian novelist, her mediating activity as a translator and reviewer of German books (e.g., David Friedrich Stauss's *The Life of Jesus, Critically Examined* (1846) and *The Essence of Christianity* (1854) by Ludwig Feuerbach) would have established her credentials as one of the most important interpreters of German culture since Thomas Carlyle's engagement with Goethe in the 1820s and 1830s. These large-scale translations contributed to the dialogue on religion that had begun at that time with the transfer of the Higher Criticism from German universities to their sister institutions in the Anglo-American world. The major essays and reviews written during Eliot's sojourn in Germany include "The Morality of Wilhelm Meister" (1855) and "The Natural History of German Life" (1856).

At a time when even rudimentary knowledge of German was still uncommon in Britain, Eliot had acquired expert skill in the language on her own. Thus, without a university education, she had accomplished what, in a famous essay, "The Function of Criticism at the Present Time," Matthew Arnold opined that the leading British writers of the nineteenth century most emphatically had not: immersion in the larger currents of European ideas.[10] As the product of a radically different cultural orientation (German vs. Greco-Roman) and literary apprenticeship (translating and reviewing)

---

10   Arnold reproaches the Romantic poets for being "uncritical," seemingly untouched by the great revolutionary ideas coming out of Germany in the wake of Immanuel Kant (1724–1804) and Goethe.

from that of her male contemporaries, Eliot was an exception to the typical intellectual insularity of male writers in Britain. Having been denied the classical education that formed the training of men and permitted only the most rudimentary schooling and superficial accomplishments, she and other leading women writers—Mary Wollstonecraft, Sarah Austin, and Margaret Fuller—nonetheless acquired an intellectual tradition of their own, based not on Latin and Greek but on contemporary German authors and ideas. Especially important in this alternative intellectual movement were German writers, poets, and philosophers. No figure was, of course, more important in this process of appropriation and domestication than Goethe, Germany's protean answer to Shakespeare, Isaac Newtown, and Charles Darwin, who combined achievements in both literature and science. Translation and other forms of literary service work comprised both an alternative education as well as an entryway into the profession of letters for women writers. Mediating Goethe thus functioned as a validating cultural platform for writers on the margins, with limited or completely obstructed access to the means of literary production and the expression of political dissent. To paraphrase Friedrich Nietzsche, as Harold Bloom does in *The Anxiety of Influence*: "When one hasn't had a good father, it is necessary to invent one."[11] Women writers in Britain had little choice but to exchange the indifferent culture of their birth for a foreign, nurturing cultural legacy. Put another way, the domestication of German culture was, for anglophone women writers, a means of acquiring cultural capital from an indifferent, even hostile dominant culture, its publishing institutions, and the reading public formed by them. In a letter to Carlyle in July 1827 Goethe intimated that the vocation of the translator as cultural intermediary is

---

11 Harold Bloom, *The Anxiety of Influence: A Theory of Poetry* (New York: Oxford University Press, 2nd Edition, 1997 [1973]), 56.

indeed sacred: "so ist jeder Übersetzer ein Prophet seinem Volke" [every translator is a prophet to his own people].[12]

Lewes could not have chosen a better collaborator when he invited Eliot to accompany him to Weimar in 1854. The pretext for the journey was to permit Lewes to research his biography of Goethe, but Germany also served as a much needed refuge and destination for an unofficial honeymoon. Once in Weimar, the couple quickly established their daily work routine: Lewes composed and Eliot polished his drafts and provided the translations from Goethe's works cited in the text. Ironically, by leaving aside her reviewing and abandoning her contacts in the London literary world and immersing herself in the writings of Goethe, Eliot acquired the wherewithal to become a novelist. The transformation of Mary Ann Evans, maid-of-all-literary-hackwork, to George Eliot, literary giant, can be attributed to what Virginia Woolf called "the great liberation which had come to her with personal happiness."[13] Indeed, it was in Weimar, in the empowering shadow of Goethe, a fellow transgressor of bourgeois morality, that Eliot achieved emotional and intellectual fulfillment. This pilgrimage to the epicenter of German culture, more than any other episode in her life, was decisive in shaping her destiny as a writer of original fiction. Weimar offered Eliot the opportunity to come into close proximity with the greatest cultural figures of the day, to escape the treadmill of translating and reviewing, and to explore new avenues of self-development. In the process, she discovered previously untapped reserves of self-confidence and ambition that inspired a radical reconstruction of her identity.

In Weimar Eliot and Lewes were welcomed in the best homes and salons, where they established lasting friendships with leading

---

12   Letter of Goethe to Carlyle, 20 July 1827, *Correspondence Between Goethe and Carlyle*, ed. Charles Eliot Norton (New York: Cooper Square Publishers, 1970), 18.

13   Virginia Woolf, "George Eliot," *Times Literary Supplement* 18 (20 November 1919): 657–658.

German cultural celebrities. Foremost among them were Ottilie von Goethe (1796–1872), the writer's daughter-in-law, the composer and pianist Franz Liszt (1811–1886), and Johann Peter Eckermann (1792–1854), Goethe's secretary. Eliot's travel journal records her surprise at being openly received in polite society in Germany, something she could never expect on their return to London. The burghers of Weimar, she learned, were incredibly tolerant of irregular personal relations. Goethe and Christiane Vulpius (1765–1816), mother of Goethe's only child, August, lived together for several years before marrying in 1806. While still married to other people, Liszt and Princess Sayn-Wittgenstein openly cohabited. Of German manners and morals Eliot noted at the time that "the Germans, to counterbalance their want of taste and politeness, are at least free from the bigotry and exclusiveness of their more refined cousins" in Britain.[14]

The sacrifice of friends and family who turned their backs on her at the news of her flight to Weimar was undoubtedly great, but Eliot may have come to deem this loss bearable because something miraculous occurred in Germany. For it was in Weimar, where she forfeited her "good name" for the sake of love, that Eliot morphed from a drudge, anonymously translating and reviewing, to a writer who would produce some of the century's greatest novels. Weimar, as it turned out, was a shape-shifting place where identities were emended, altered, and exchanged. Goethe had managed a similar trick, metamorphosing from the author of *Werther*, the ultimate adolescent primal scream, to emerge as Europe's last true polymath and the nineteenth century's preeminent man of letters. In contrast to Eliot's native Britain, which was, as Samuel Johnson and John Keats lamented, a conspicuously poor mother to her literary offspring, Germany was the incubator of genius, who nurtured her poets while tolerating their foibles.

---

14   George Eliot, "Recollections of Berlin 1854–1855," *The Journals of George Eliot*, ed. Margaret Harris and Judith Johnston (Cambridge: Cambridge UP, 1998), 258.

Of all the geniuses based in Weimar or whose ghostly presence could still be felt in the picturesque town, Goethe exercised the
most far-reaching influence on Eliot's fiction, and, with *Middlemarch*, she returned to her roots, the intellectual atmosphere and the
preoccupations of her "Weimar period." The best clue to Eliot's
emulation of Goethe in *Middlemarch* is her use of Goethe's novel
Wilhelm Meister's Apprenticeship (1795–96) as a template for her
greatest novel. During her sojourn in Weimar Eliot experienced
firsthand the German idealization of the artist. It was thus in Germany that untitled and penniless Ladislaws could become genuine
rather than alienated Shelleys and Byrons. In *Middlemarch* Eliot ad-
dresses the characteristic dilemma confronted by the *Bildungsroman*
[novel of personal growth]: to represent the development of a complex personality at a time when the aristocratic values are being
threatened by an increasingly industrialized capitalism and mass
democracy. Following Goethe's example in *Wilhelm Meister*, Eliot
poses the problem to be confronted by her protagonists: can an individual still be the architect of their own experience? Can circum-
stances be altered to allow for the realization of epic ambitions? Can
Dorothea Brooke, Tertius Lydgate, or Will Ladislaw bridge the divide between what is given and what can be achieved by sheer will-
power or fantasy?

Initially, it seems that Dorothea's task is identical to Wilhelm
Meister's: to discover the validity of the reality of this world while
reconciling the poetry of the heart with the outer conditions of life
as both of them seek their way in murky moral universe. But this
course of action, the conventional arc of the *Bildungsroman* plotline,
turns out to be an utter impossibility for Dorothea. As a result, she
is incapable of altering her social milieu. Instead, it changes her,
obliterating her idealism and thwarting her epic ambitions. Rather
than affording Dorothea opportunities for self-realization in altruistic schemes, the social pressures inherent in Middlemarch clipped
her wings just as surely as they corrupted the novel's Icarus figure,
Ladislaw, by turning him into a fortune hunter. The possibility of

finding personal happiness in a conventional marriage, if not in heroic martyrdom, was an option Eliot herself was never given. The conclusion of *Middlemarch* therefore reflects a fantasy of the author, who could not overcome her status as a pariah in British society.

Ultimately, *Middlemarch* embodies a rejection of the definition of *Bildung* established in Goethe's *Wilhelm Meister*, where we see the formation of the protagonist up to the moment when he ceases to be egoistic and becomes socially centered and begins to shape the self for altruistic purposes. For example, Wilhelm ultimately gives up the wandering life of an itinerant actor to become a physician. But in the world of Eliot's novel such growth is not attainable. The mere selection of St. Theresa of Avila as the novel's emblem or dedicatee, a powerful example of thought and feeling translated into significant action, anticipates Dorothea's ultimate failure and suggests that the novel is, in fact, an anti-*Bildungsroman*. The implication is, of course, that the epic life is no longer possible in the modern world of early Victorian Britain. As indicated in the novel's denouement, all that remains for Dorothea is withdrawal from society.

Another element of the new social reality that is explored in *Middlemarch* is the emergence of the modern intelligentsia as a distinct class. Represented by Will Ladislaw, this new class is severed from power and alienated from respectable society. In contrast to Dorothea, Will, a figure who walks straight out of German Romanticism into the harsh light of a realistic novel, is the true, classic *Bildungsroman* protagonist as well as Eliot's homage to Goethe's eponymous Wilhelm. Unlike Dorothea or Lydgate, whose philanthropic vocations are well established, Will's pathway remains in formation. He is still seeking the proper outlet for his talents, and his experimentation runs the gamut from pursuing art in Rome to dabbling in local politics as Mr. Brooke's campaign manager and press attaché. His development is, however, interrupted when he falls in love with Dorothea and embarks on a conventional family life. As a consequence, Will exchanges the questing pursuit of a meaningful

life for the settled, trivial existence of a bourgeois, a fate incompatible with his previous identity "as a kind of Shelley" or "a Byronic
hero."

As crucial as interacting with Goethe's works was to Eliot's
emergence as a novelist, in *Middlemarch* we see that Goethe's
worldview and the values associated with it (which emphasize individual growth from self-absorption into sympathetic beneficence) are not suited for the new age dominated by opportunistic
cynics like Bulstrode and their collaborators like Lydgate. Goethe,
the enabler of the rise of an alternative culture that would challenge
the patriarchy for literary supremacy, had a hand in fostering the
enduring achievement of Wollstonecraft, Fuller, and Eliot—among
his chief British and American admirers. Their origins as cultural
outsiders and the vehicle of their rise to fame—mediating Goethe—
may have been obscured by time, but it bears remembering how
such unlikely alliances yielded such a rich literary harvest.